Generational Wealth

ISBN-10: 1456492918
EAN-13: 9781456492915

Generational Wealth

Business & Investing Guide to Building an Empire

2011-2012 Edition

LaFoy Orlando Thomas III, Esq.

Contents

Chapter I

Introduction

The need for education on business and investing has never been more important than it is today. As evidenced by the Great Recession, the name that many economists have dubbed the most recent economic downturn, which required a massive government stimulus package to prevent economic catastrophe, those who are financially savvy usually are the ones that benefit most from calamity and famine. Not to mention are usually the ones who prosper most in expanding economies as well.

Whether it is in real estate, stocks, or investing your life savings into a small business, positioning our money in an environment where it can grow is a necessity if wealth is to be attained.

The difference in investing philosophies between the financially sophisticated and everyone else can sometimes be compared to two farmers. The first farmer is wise and plants his seeds in good soil because he knows he will reap a very large harvest that will allow him to eat and replant his seeds on a continual basis for the rest of his life.

The second farmer wasn't raised or educated with the same principles as the first farmer. Instead of planting his seeds in good soil, he decides to hide some of his seeds under his mattress while throwing the rest in the garbage. As time passes, the seeds under his mattress aren't as valuable as they were before and no longer can produce all of the fruits and vegetables that they could have if planted originally.

This analogy is very similar to what happens today between those who are financially savvy and everyone else. People with aspirations to become rich consistently spend their money on assets that will continually bring positive cash flow. On the other hand, many of those without a basic education in business or finance will often spend their hard earned money on futile possessions that have little to no chance of an appreciated resale value.

It is my hope that this book's influence will lead to more business owners and investors, who will play a large part in producing jobs and stimulating the economy.

I can't stress how important it is to do something positive with your hard earned money before you decide to spend it on futile possessions, such as luxury cars and fine jewelry. It's not that you can't have these nice things, but I'm only suggesting that you don't spend your hard earned money to get them. Instead, spend your hard earned money on an asset, like a nice piece of real estate that has a continual positive cash flow that you can then spend however you please.

The key is to first put your money in an environment where it can continue to grow and spit more seeds out. On the other hand, if you neglect buying appreciating or income producing assets, the opportunity for harvest doesn't exist, and the seeds are practically thrown in the garbage.

Chapter 2

The Importance of Economics

How well a particular investment performs is generally influenced by the state of the economy. Before learning about a specific investment, it is essential to learn about the economy and the impact it has on the world of investing. Also, it is very important to know what economic cycle you are in and know how to adjust and react to each climate accordingly.

The economy is measured by several economic indicators that take the temperature of the economy, and some indicators even give a future forecast on what is expected of the economy in the future.

Of all the economic indicators, some are more important than others. The most important economic indicator is considered by many as the parent indicator, and that is the gross domestic product (GDP). The GDP is the total dollar value of all goods and services produced by labor and property in the United States.

A GDP that is increasing signifies an economic growth cycle that may cause inflation, and a GDP on the decline signifies an economy that is slowing down and may have the potential to cause deflation. Inflation is the rise of prices for goods and services; deflation is the decrease in prices for goods and services.

The GDP report measures quarterly activity and has a heavy influence on how people invest and spend their money. The report is released three times each quarter, being revised each time to finally come up with a final report for the quarter during the last month of the next quarter. For example, the final revision of the GDP report for the first quarter (January-March) would be released in

June and can be found on the Yahoo! Finance page with all the other indicators.

Keeping track of the GDP growth (or decline) numbers should give you a good feel for the state of the economy and also let you know what phase of the business or economic cycle you are currently in. There are generally five phases in the business cycle as outlined below.

Business/Economic Cycle

1.) **Downturn:** Starting from the peak in the economy, the downturn starts when the GDP has its first quarter of negative growth and lasts for as long as the GDP report is signifying negative growth. Two consecutive quarters of negative GDP growth is officially considered a recession. During a downturn, investors generally get nervous and begin to dump quality investments for less than market value. At this time, investment bargains are usually easy to come by.

2.) **Trough:** The trough signifies the end of the downturn or recession. It represents the lowest level in the business cycle. During a trough, because it is the lowest phase in the cycle, reports start to improve and the economy is getting ready to bounce back. In my opinion, this is the best time to invest, especially in real estate and stocks. Due to a lack of consumer confidence at this point in the cycle, investments are usually at their lowest point. Once you're at the bottom, the only way you can go is up, so I advise you to buy all the quality real estate and stocks as possible.

3.) **Recovery:** The recovery begins when the GDP growth is positive again. The recovery is over when the GDP level surpasses the previous peak in the previous business cycle, which indicates the start of an expansion.

4.) **Expansion:** An expansion occurs when the GDP rate is reaching new heights and continues until it reaches a new peak. At this point, investments normally are costing more than they are really worth. During this phase of the cycle, be careful in what you buy because the peak is coming and on its way. If you buy too close to the top, you may have to sell on the way back down, which will possibly result in a loss.

5.) **Peak:** The peak is the highest point in the business cycle. In my opinion, this is the worst time to start investing because once you're at the top, the only way you can go is down.

Now that we have a good understanding of the economic cycle, we can now go into depth on the most important economic reports that generally give you a clue in what direction the economy is headed before the GDP report is even released.

Although there are many economic indicators viewed and adhered to by Wall Street, there are only six of them besides the GDP report that I find important, and they are listed below. It is important to understand that most economic indicators are subject to monthly revisions; therefore, be aware that the GDP reading is not the only indicator that is subject to changes once more data is received by the source of the economic report.

Important Economic Indicators

1.) **Consumer Price Index (CPI):** The CPI measures the level of inflation or increase in prices for goods and services in the marketplace. Inflation is generally high during times of an expansion and lower during a downturn. During an expansion, people are spending money at new levels, and the high demand for goods and services generally allows businesses to raise their prices. Generally, when inflation is growing too rapidly, the Federal Reserve (Federal Open Market Committee) will take action and raise interest rates, which will make money not as easy to borrow, which slows down the crazy shopping and in turn slows down inflation. The CPI report is released monthly, approximately two weeks after the month ends.

2.) **Employment Report:** The employment report contains information such as the unemployment rate, payrolls, and hourly wages. This report is very important as it is one of the first indicators each month of which direction the economy is going. In times of an expansion or growing economy, payrolls are usually up, and the unemployment rate is usually down and vice versa for times of a downturn or a recession. As was the case during the Great Recession, when consumers are out of work, the economy suffers because of it. This report is also released monthly on the first Friday of every month.

3.) **Retail Sales:** The retail sales report is one of the most important reports as it gives us a good indication of quarterly consumer spending, which accounts for approximately 70% of the gross domestic product. Generally, when retail sales are up, inflation shortly follows as it shows an increased demand for consumer goods. This report is usually released in the middle of every month.

4.) **Consumer Confidence:** The Consumer Confidence Index gives a reflection of how consumers feel about the current and future state of the economy or business cycle. A decrease in consumer confidence usually causes a decrease in retail sales and, therefore, a decrease in the GDP. When consumers are not comfortable about the current or future state of the economy, they usually tighten their belts and decrease their level of spending due to worries that hard times may be coming ahead. During an expansion (good times), consumer confidence is generally high as the job market is generally good and many investments will have reached new highs. The consumer confidence report usually comes out the last week of every month.

5.) **Housing Starts:** Along with the employment and retail sales reports, the housing starts report is one of the most important. The housing starts report details the number of single and multi-family homes being built. As we all know, when a home is built and then purchased, it calls for further spending on appliances, fixtures, and other household related goods. This report gives us a pretty solid indication of where the economy is going approximately three to six months ahead of time. The housing starts report is released monthly around the middle of the month and is heavily watched by Wall Street.

6.) **Durable Goods:** Durable goods can be described as items with a life expectancy of at least two to three years. Durable goods would include such items as washers, dryers, stoves, computers, and other long lasting items bought by consumers and businesses alike. Durable good sales are generally up in an expanding economy and down in times of downturn and recession. This report is also released monthly, approximately three weeks after the reporting month ends.

Supply & Demand

One of the most important, yet simple, aspects of economics is supply and demand. Generally, when the supply of something is high and the demand for it is low, the price for that item generally declines. When the supply of something is low and the demand for it is high, prices generally increase since there are more buyers than product available.

This situation is very evident in today's society. For example, when the demand for gas or housing goes up, the price usually goes up with it, especially if the demand increases in comparison with supply.

On the other hand, if the demand for something is low at Walmart or Target and the supply of that item is high, the item usually goes on clearance to entice shoppers to buy.

This also is the case when department stores have clearance sales to get rid of old trends or fashions that are no longer demanding the attention of consumers. An example of this would be in the winter season and summer clothes are marked down to their lowest points. This is because the demand for summer clothes is very low in the winter time and, therefore, need an extremely low price to entice consumers.

Another scenario is when the demand and supply of something is approximately equal. This is considered the equilibrium point, and prices generally stay the same except for some minor adjustments due to inflation.

The Federal Reserve

The Federal Reserve System, which was created by Congress in 1913, is the central bank for the United States. As the country's central bank, it acts as a bank for the government and for other banks. The Federal Reserve System is comprised of the Board of Governors, 12 regional Federal Reserve Banks, and a number of branches that are supervised by the Board of Governors.

The Federal Reserve Board of Governors has seven members who are appointed by the president and confirmed by the Senate. Board members serve terms of 14 years, which are staggered; therefore, every even-numbered year a member's term shall expire. After serving a full term, Board members may not be reappointed; however, if a Board member is appointed and confirmed to finish the term of a resigning member, he or she may later be appointed to a full term. The chairman and vice chairman of the Board serve four-year terms and may be reappointed after their terms expire as long as they are still Board members.

In my opinion, the two most important duties of the Federal Reserve System are creating and implementing the nation's monetary policy and supervising and regulating banks. The most significant goals of monetary policy are to ensure price stability, high employment, and economic growth.

Federal Open Market Committee

The Federal Open Market Committee, which is a part of the Federal Reserve System, is responsible for setting monetary policy and consists of the seven-member Board of Governors, the president of the Federal Reserve Bank of New York, and four of the remaining 11 Reserve Bank presidents, who serve on a rotating schedule; therefore, there are 12 members on this committee at all times. The Board of Governors and the New York Reserve Bank president always serve on the Federal Open Market Committee.

The 11 Reserve Bank presidents who rotate serve one-year terms on the committee.

It is important to note that all of the Reserve Bank presidents are allowed to attend committee meetings and participate in discussions; however, only five in any given year are allowed to vote. Committee membership changes at the first regularly scheduled meeting of the year. Currently in 2011, the members are New York, Chicago, Philadelphia, Dallas, and Minneapolis. In 2012, the members will be New York, Cleveland, Richmond, Atlanta, and San Francisco. In 2013, the members will be New York, Chicago, Boston, St. Louis, and Kansas City.

The Federal Open Market Committee holds eight regularly scheduled meetings each year in Washington, D.C. During these meetings, there is generally a discussion on the state of the economy and a vote is taken whether or not to change its target for the federal funds rate.

Federal Funds Rate

Banks are required to maintain a certain level of funds (or reserves) that cannot be loaned out to borrowers. Such reserves can be kept in vault or with Federal Reserve Banks. The Board of Governors (and not the Federal Open Market Committee) has sole control over setting reserve requirements. When a bank is not in compliance with the required reserve amount, it can take a loan from the Federal Reserve or from another bank.

The federal funds rate is the interest rate that banks charge each other for overnight loans. The actual rate at which banks charge each other is negotiated between the two banks, and the Federal Reserve uses open market operations to have semi-control over this key rate. The Federal Open Market Committee uses its ability to buy and sell government securities to increase or decrease the nation's money supply.

When the Federal Open Market Committee wishes to raise interest rates, it will sell government securities to decrease the nation's money supply. This, in turn, discourages banks from placing themselves in a position to need to borrow money and will cause them to loan out less to bank customers. When the Federal Open Market Committee wishes to lower interest rates, it will buy government securities, which increases the nation's money supply. This, in turn, encourages banks to lend more, which leads to increased spending by consumers and businesses alike.

Discount Rate

The discount rate, which is controlled by the Board of Governors, is the interest rate that the Federal Reserve charges banks for short-term loans. Although not currently, the discount rate is usually set at approximately 1 percentage point above the federal funds rate. Since banks can procure loans from other banks at the federal funds rate, a loan from the Federal Reserve at the discount rate is basically a tool of last resort for banking institutions seeking to raise short-term capital.

Last Words of Chapter

Having your finger on the pulse of the economy is critical if you are going to have long-term success with investing or if you plan on having a successful business operation.

Generally, in times of a bad market or downturn, most businesses decrease their spending and tighten their belts as much as possible. As stated by Robert Kiyosaki, during times of a bad market, I think that extra spending should be done on advertising and other marketing to give your business or product as much exposure as possible.

During hard times, the more you cut costs which bring in business for you and generate sales, the more your business is going to suffer and sales are going to decrease.

When investing, it is unwise to buy real estate or stocks at inflated prices during the high points of an expansion or peak in the economy, but without the proper education, one can't possible know what is considered a good or bad time in the economy.

On the other hand, I recommend buying underpriced real estate and stocks during bad times and holding them until the market recovers. During the hard times in the economy, people are often scared and make decisions based on that emotion and sell very good investments for much less than they are worth.

Likewise, when the economy is strong, people are more than willing to buy overinflated investments because they always think it can only get better, forgetting the last recession that took place only a few years earlier.

I believe it was Warren Buffett who said it best, "Be greedy when others are fearful and fearful when others are greedy."

Chapter 3

Real Estate Investing: The Basics & Beyond

In the world of investing, there are practically hundreds, if not thousands, of different investment options for an investor to choose from. Often, many people are advised that the best investment choices are in various stocks or mutual funds. Although it can be true at times, such as during our current economic conditions where we have had a credit crunch, it is typically not the case.

Generally, when you question someone who makes this type of statement, he will tell you how stocks have grown, on average, approximately 10% annually over the last 75 years and so on and so forth. In many cases, investing in stocks can be a good decision to help add diversity to your portfolio, but in no way should it be the main piece of your investment puzzle during normal credit conditions. The reason why stocks shouldn't be the center of your portfolio is the huge benefit you get from investing in real estate called leverage.

Before I begin discussing the wealth strategies on real estate investing, I must advise you that some of what is written between chapters three and four regarding real estate financing is based on a normal, free-flowing credit environment. As you may be aware, due to the real estate bubble burst and subsequent credit crunch, we have not had a normal, free-flowing credit environment since the start of the financial crisis and may not see one again until 2012. However, it is important to note that it is possible that the current conditions may very well become the new standard.

Although I don't believe that the mortgage industry will return to identical operations as before the Great Recession, I do predict that once the economy returns close to full strength, credit will again be easy to obtain, including mortgages.

As of February 2011, 100% financing is very hard to come by. Unless you qualify for a VA loan, it can be almost impossible to qualify for 100% financing. The closest thing to 100% financing that a first-time homebuyer can expect in today's economy is an F.H.A. loan, which only requires a 3.5% down payment as long as the borrower has a credit score above 580. F.H.A. borrowers with credit scores between 500 and 579 will be required to have down payments of 10%. In today's economy, many lenders are even requiring a 20% down payment for loans that are considered jumbo (loans over $417,000). Commercial real estate lenders are also requiring much larger down payments than before the Great Recession.

Real Property and Personal Property

Property can be divided between real property and personal property. Real property is land and anything permanently attached to it, such as trees, buildings, and anything permanently attached to the building. Personal property would be items such as clothes, DVD players, kitchen tables, and anything else that's not directly or indirectly permanently attached to land.

The good thing about real estate is that you can touch it. If you have the address, you can drive by and see what type of condition the property is in without having to be a real estate genius. On the other hand, if you are not financially literate in advanced finance concepts, trying to figure out if a stock or company is in good shape can be almost impossible.

Banks understand this very well, and this is one of the main reasons why they won't hesitate to give someone with a good credit and employment background all of the money that he needs for a real estate investment. However, they would look at the same A-credit borrower like he has lost his mind if he came in asking for a loan of any size to buy stocks.

This isn't meant to be a bashing of stocks because like I said, stocks can be a very valuable piece to a solid portfolio. My purpose here is to separate and put a magnifying glass on the two and show the large difference in benefits between them. Investing in real estate has an enormous advantage over investing in publicly traded stocks, and I feel this is one of the many things that you must know about real estate.

Buying Your First Home: The Basics

Buying your first home can be a very challenging and mentally draining experience. This is, of course, if you aren't aware ahead of time of everything that is required of you and everything that you will be forced to go through in order to complete the process.

However, it is an experience that you should be happy to go through. It is one of the best ways to build wealth in this country as the net worth of a homeowner is usually much higher than someone who is not a homeowner.

This is because when a home increases in value as it usually does in healthy real estate markets, it creates equity for the homeowner. Equity is the difference between what the home is worth and what you owe the mortgage lender. For example, let's say you have a home that is now worth $200,000, and you owe the mortgage lender $150,000. The $50,000 difference between the $200,000 it's worth and $150,000 you owe is considered equity, and that equity is your portion of real ownership in the home.

When a person sells a home, after the mortgage lender is paid off, the remaining money goes to the seller of the home, and it doesn't need to be shared with anyone, not even the bank that may have loaned him 95% of the money to purchase the property.

Generally, in any business agreement, when someone provides the start-up money of any amount, it is generally expected for that investor to receive a percentage of the profits. However, in real estate there is no such expectation. When all things are considered, I firmly believe that real estate is the best investment out there for the individual investor.

Before you start looking to buy your first home, it is important to make sure that your credit is intact. The better your credit, the lower the interest rate you will qualify for, so this is very important as it can save you tens of thousands of dollars over the life of the loan.

This doesn't mean that you must have perfect credit. It just means that you should make sure during the last 12 to 24 months leading up to your home purchase that you don't have any 30-day late payments on any of your lines of credit that appear on your credit report.

If a person is late by 10 or 15 days on a credit account, it doesn't usually hurt his credit report as your report only shows blemishes for payments that are not paid at all or for those that were paid greater than 30 days late.

Lines of credit that generally report monthly to the credit bureaus would include mortgages, car loans, credit cards, student loans, and any other revolving or installment credit you may have. Generally, the electric, gas, and water companies do not report to the credit agencies unless you become so delinquent that your account is sent to collections, which also isn't good if you are looking to buy a house soon.

Once you've done a good job in securing a good credit profile, it is wise to start shopping for the best mortgage lender for your situation. It is important to know that all lenders are not created equal; therefore, it is important to do your due diligence and find the best one for your particular situation. One lender may have a better program for perfect credit, while another may have the best program for fair or good credit.

In the process of shopping for a loan, it is important to know your credit score ahead of time, so when companies give you quotes, they don't have to pull your credit, which knocks your score down a few points with each pull.

Once you find a lender that you are comfortable with, you should ask to be pre-approved so you can know how much of a home you can actually afford. After you get pre-approved, you should then find a good realtor in your local area.

It is very important **not** to find a realtor before you find a lender because many realtors are notorious for referring you to their business sharing mortgage buddy down the street that may not be in your best interest.

In my opinion, at least 50% of all realtors have a mortgage lender whom they trade business with even if they know that the homebuyer could get a much better deal elsewhere. In return, realtors expect their mortgage buddies to refer to them all business that goes to them first, which isn't as bad because you as the homebuyer won't pay the realtor anyway.

Your realtor is paid from the commission that the seller agreed to pay his realtor when he listed his home for sale. The way it works is, if your agent brings you, as a buyer to the seller, the commission that would have went solely to the selling agent is now split between the two agents 50/50 unless some other agreement has been worked out.

The average selling realtor's commission ranges from 5 to 8 percent depending on how good the realtor is and how hard he or she believes it will be to sell the home. To give you a clearer picture of how this works, let's say a realtor's commission is 6%, and the selling price is $200,000. The total commission for selling this house would be $12,000. If two agents are involved (buyer's and seller's agent), the $12,000 commission would be split between the two agents 50/50, each agent getting $6,000 in commission.

Once you find a good realtor that you are comfortable with, you can start looking for a home. It is of the essence that you like the realtor that you choose as you will be spending a lot of time with him or her riding around looking at houses. In many cases, your realtor will become your temporary best friend as you will begin to see him or her day and night with phone conversations and emails seeming routine until you find your home.

While looking at various homes, it is a good idea to visit the area at different times during the day to get a good feel for the true identity of the neighborhood. While visiting the neighborhood, it is always a good idea to knock on doors and ask questions about the neighborhood.

From my past experiences, most of the elderly neighbors will be more than willing to tell you everything they know about the neighborhood, which will generally be some very helpful information for you and help you to decide if that is an area where you really want to live.

Once you find a home that you are interested in, you and your realtor would then prepare an offer for the home. Most offers are made with several common contingencies to protect the potential buyer: contingent upon financing, appraisal exceeding the purchase price, and inspection being approved by the buyer within 10 days.

Generally, a good realtor will have the inside scoop on what the bottom line is and what the seller is willing to accept for the home. Realtors usually get this information from the seller's agent as they will both do all that they can to work together and sell the home.

This can be seen as very disloyal as a seller is under the impression that everything that he discusses in secrecy with his agent is kept confidential between the two of them. This is generally not the case as both agents will share information with each other, from the seller's agent telling the bottom line that the seller will take for the home, and the buyer's agent will generally share the maximum dollar amount that the buyer is willing to pay for a particular property.

With that said, please don't expect anyone in a real estate transaction to be entirely on your side, not even yourself. If a person doesn't have his emotions in check before going into a real estate transaction, his emotions will normally influence the buying decision, which may lead a normally logical person into making an emotion based, irrational decision.

When making an offer on a home, it is best to offer slightly under the amount that your realtor has told you is the seller's bottom line, while at the same time asking the seller to pay some of your closing costs.

For example, if the listing price is $265,000, and your realtor told you that the seller's bottom line is $240,000, you should offer $230,000 with the seller paying $6,900 of your closing costs.

In many cases, the seller will accept this offer as it is close to what he wanted and his realtor will put a little pressure on him to do so. At this point, the seller will accept, reject, or make a counter-offer.

If the seller rejects your offer, you can make another offer closer to what he is asking for the home in hopes that he will accept. If he makes a counter-offer, he will generally ask for more money, and in most cases, the two parties will find a way to meet in the middle.

In any case, once you have a purchase and sell agreement is when the ball starts rolling. At this point, you would order an inspection and then approve or disapprove what the report reveals. Generally, no inspection report comes back perfect, and whatever flaws that are found can be used to your advantage to negotiate a lower price on the home.

After all of the final kinks are worked out with the inspection report, you then contact your mortgage lender and let it know that you have a purchase and sell agreement on a home. At this time, you would complete an application online or over the phone and lock in your interest rate and closing costs.

You will then need to send in verification of pay stubs, bank statements, W2's, and potentially any other income or asset verification needed. You will also be required to sign some mortgage disclosures that include a Good Faith Estimate (GFE) and a Truth in Lending Statement.

After all of this information is received by the lender, it will generally order the appraisal for your home. The appraiser will do research on similar homes that have sold in the area of the home you're buying and examine the home to come up with an approximate value of the property.

This process usually goes smoothly, but in some cases, you may find out that the seller is overcharging for the home and the appraised value may come back less than what the seller is willing to sell it for. In most situations, the lender will not be willing to fund the mortgage for this home.

If the seller is not willing to renegotiate, it is usually a deal breaker, but in most cases, sellers are reasonable and will do what they need to do to sell the home.

Simultaneously, when the appraisal is ordered, the mortgage company will order your title work to make sure that the seller is the actual legal owner of the home and that there are no defects in title that materially affect the value of the property. Also, the mortgage company will do an employment verification to make sure you're actively employed as you stated in your application.

If all of this information comes back fine, your file will be submitted for underwriting. The underwriter will double check everything in the file and give a last say of yes or no, or in some cases, he or she will say yes upon certain conditions. A common condition may be that the buyer has to pay off certain collection accounts before closing. Whatever the case, after final approval from the underwriter, the file is sent to the closing department and the date of your closing is scheduled.

One of the last things that you must perform before closing is setting up your homeowners insurance. Generally, you will have to pay one year's worth of insurance up-front with your insurance company, which usually will cost between $600 and $1,500, depending on the size, value, and location of the home.

One thing I highly recommend is using the same company that you have your car insurance with as your agent will normally give you a sizeable discount on both for doing so.

The closing is the final stage in the home buying process and can sometimes be the most mentally draining and demanding. At closing, you will often meet the sellers of the home unless they signed ahead of time. This is also where you literally get to read and sign over 50 forms.

It is very important to make sure that the interest rate and closing costs that you agreed to with your mortgage lender are what you are signing for at closing. It is very normal for the lender to offer you a good rate and low closing costs in order to win your business and then switch them both on you at closing.

If this happens to you, I recommend walking away from the closing table without signing anything. This is what the mortgage industry calls the "bait and switch." Don't go for it as this is very unethical and deserves to be walked away from.

On the other hand, if everything is as agreed to, you will literally spend hours reviewing and signing papers before finally being handed keys to your new home. At this point, you are now considered a homeowner and can begin receiving the benefits of homeownership that are plentiful.

Although this may have been a long, tiring process, it is definitely worth it. Once you go to your new home, it is always good to introduce yourself to all of your new neighbors, especially those that are right next to you.

Investing in Real Estate

As stated before, real estate is a great investment. No other investment out there has the benefits of real estate or even comes close for that matter. There are many ways to begin a career investing in real estate, and there are many different types of properties that a person can invest in.

The most common investment is in residential real estate. Generally, when a person takes this route, he buys single-family or two-family homes to begin with and then moves up as his experience or financial situation gets better.

The best way to show you how this works is to illustrate a scenario of a person who begins a career investing in real estate. I will walk you through as she moves from one property to the next, using some very good techniques to get the absolute best mortgage possible.

The story I'm going to walk you through is the story of a woman named Michelle. When Michelle graduated from Emory University in Atlanta, GA, with a double major in business and communications, she immediately got a job at a large Fortune 500 company as the assistant sales director.

Her new job came with a comfortable salary of $50,000 and a chance for a yearly bonus of between $5,000 and $25,000 depending upon the performance of her department, which she oversaw. Being a hard worker for Michelle was inherent, so she knew she could motivate her team to the highest level possible.

After saving money to build a security nest for six months, she purchased her first home that had three bedrooms, two bathrooms, and a two-car garage, 10 minutes from Downtown Atlanta for $135,000. She bought the home with little money down and got a pretty good mortgage since she let the mortgage lender know that she intended to "owner occupy" the home.

Her total PITI (principal, interest, taxes, and insurance) payment was only $1,025, which left her with plenty of extra cash each month to save for her next investment. Although she liked this home a lot, she didn't plan on living in it for long, and she wanted to turn it into an investment property and move up to a slightly bigger house to live in.

After a year of living in her first home, Michelle hired a real estate agent to help her find her next home to buy that she was going to live in. Her realtor advised her that the best way to turn her current home into an investment property would be to hire a reputable property management company.

The realtor informed Michelle that for a small percentage of rents collected that the property management company would collect rents, pay any bills related to the property, handle any evictions if needed, and schedule all maintenance and repairs. She thought this was a good idea as she assumed that the downside to investing in real estate was going to be receiving calls at 3:00 a.m. about the hot water heater not working.

Using a property management company erased that concern and increased Michelle's chances of collecting rents on time each month as tenants are more likely to pay a company on time than they would a person (the homeowner) that they might not even like.

After hiring a property management company to take care of the property, she focused solely on finding her next home that would ultimately become an investment one day.

After looking for about three weeks, Michelle had a purchase and sale agreement on a nice home about 15 minutes from Downtown Atlanta for $155,000. The home had three bedrooms, three bathrooms, and a two-car garage, very similar to her first home. In addition to the three normal conditions in the contract (conditioned upon financing, appraisal, and inspection), she also added a condition that stated that her current home needed to be rented out with a one-year lease before closing. This covered her end as she didn't want to be stuck paying two mortgages.

She hired a very good property management company that was able to rent out her current home approximately three weeks before closing on her new home. The rent being charged for her home was $1,150, which was enough to cover PITI and the 8% charge to cover property management fees, so she was in pretty good shape to move forward.

After she closed on her new home, she became very excited about how the real estate business worked and made a commitment to find her next home within a year from the day of closing on her second home.

Less than a year after moving into her new home, she hired her current property management company to find a tenant for her current home as she was ready to make her next move up and buy her third property.

Before Michelle had a chance to call the realtor, the property management company already had a qualified tenant who was ready to move in within 30 days. This caused Michelle and her agent to speed things up and look for that next property with extreme urgency.

Due to working with Michelle on her two prior home purchases, her realtor had a good idea of what type of home she wanted and they found their next home in seven days. Purchasing this home didn't go as smoothly as the other two as her mortgage guy told her that her debt to income ratio was getting too high and that she would have to keep the mortgage under $140,000.

This is where the second problem came in at. The mortgage lender told Michelle that by her buying a property that was worth less than her current home, the underwriter would automatically assume that this was an investment property as there was no good, logical reason for her to step down in home size except for one.

Her mortgage lender told her that the only logical excuse that the underwriter was likely to accept was that the third home that she was going to buy was going to be closer to her employer than her current home.

So this meant that Michelle would be forced to buy a home that was closer to her job than her current home was, or she would be forced to get the mortgage based on an investment property that would have a much higher interest rate, higher closing costs, and larger down payment requirement. She didn't want to pay investment property rates and did the smart thing and found a home that was about 10 minutes closer to her employer than her current home was.

After she bought her third home, she decided to put a hold to her real estate purchases and wanted to grow some equity in her current homes so she could sell and move on to bigger and better investments.

She waited for about two years watching her property values dramatically increase. Purchasing homes so close to downtown really paid off. After two years, her first home that she purchased for $135,000 was now worth $180,000. The second home she bought for $155,000 was now worth $200,000, and the third home that she purchased for $140,000 was now worth $190,000.

Altogether she had over $140,000 worth of equity combined in her three homes. She decided to sell all three homes with the same realtor that she had purchased the homes with, who in return gave her a discount and sold her homes for her at a partial rate of 4%.

Due to the areas being as hot as they were, all three homes sold within four months and gave Michelle over $110,000 after all fees and closing costs were paid. At each closing, Michelle's smile became bigger and bigger as she knew that she was headed toward financial security.

Before she completed the sale and closing of her last home, she had a nice home with four bedrooms, three bathrooms, and a three-car garage under contract for $300,000 that had a mortgage payment of just under $2,000 when combined with taxes and insurance.

She bought this home with little money down and with plans of living in it for a while as she now wanted to focus on larger residential real estate, specifically small to mid-size apartment buildings.

She first tried to get pre-approved for a commercial loan with her current loan officer, but he informed her that his company couldn't finance any buildings over four units and recommended her to a good commercial lender that he knew and previously sent past customers to.

Michelle had over $160,000 at the time she met with the commercial lender, who was very impressed with Michelle's ability to build such a large nest egg only a few years after college.

After reviewing her credit and verifying her employment, the lender approved Michelle for a $500,000 commercial loan as long as she put down a minimum of 20% of her own money at closing.

The lender then referred her to a good commercial real estate agent that he shared business with. The lender assured Michelle that the realtor would be able to get her top quality for her money, which he wasn't lying about.

The first building that the realtor showed Michelle was a 20-unit apartment building 10 minutes from Downtown Atlanta. The building was appraised at over $600,000, but the realtor knew the selling realtor and got the word on it before it officially became a listing.

The seller was willing to accept $525,000 for the property as long as Michelle could get financing lined up and close within 45 days. To his surprise, Michelle was already ahead of the game and had a pre-approval letter in her back pocket.

Michelle made a formal offer in writing for $525,000, and the seller gladly accepted. Three days after they came to an agreement on the sale price, Michelle did the wise thing and had the property inspected. This was very expensive as the building had 20 units, but it was well worth the cost.

During the inspection, the inspector discovered several problems with the plumbing and electricity in several units and estimated the repair to cost over $15,000. After hearing this news, Michelle got excited as she knew that she could further use this information to her advantage.

After discussing her concerns of the inspection with the seller, she was able to do a final negotiation on the price and ended up getting the building for $490,000. She then put down 20%, which was slightly less than $100,000 and had approximately $15,000 in closing costs.

While signing her share of paperwork at the closing table, Michelle couldn't stop smiling as she saw her net worth increase by over $100,000 in a matter of hours. This was a big move for her as the building brought in an average of $600 per unit for a total gross income of $12,000. Her mortgage on the property was less than $4,500 and after all expenses were paid, gave her a net monthly profit of slightly over $6,000.

She then used this income to pay for her current mortgage on the home that she was living in as well as pay for a Mercedes Benz for $62,000 that had a monthly note of $1,500.

The income that she was receiving from her apartment building gave her more than enough income to support a very comfortable lifestyle, not including the solid income that she was getting with her current employer. At this point, she was basically living off of assets and enjoying herself while doing so.

Although Michelle put herself in a very good position financially, she wasn't close to satisfied as she went on to purchase three more apartment buildings in less than two years. With rental income and steady promotions at work, her financial situation became very comfortable and she was able to quit her job and attend graduate school at Cornell University in New York.

She was studying to get her MBA in Hotel Management as she wanted her next step to be in hotel ownership. She knew that in two years when she graduated that she would be able to sell some of her apartment buildings for very nice profits, which could potentially work as a great down payment on a mid-level hotel.

While in school, Michelle was given the opportunity to work several internships at very reputable hotel franchises, which gave her first hand experience in the hotel business. Since Michelle had a very nice income from her investments that she made back home, she didn't have to work and so she spent all of her time in graduate school studying and learning all she could about the hotel business.

After graduating with her MBA in Hotel Management from one of the top hospitality schools in the country, she was on a mission to take the Atlanta hotel scene by storm and she sold three of her apartment buildings for a profit of $575,000. With the financial condition that she was in, as well as her internationally respected MBA from Cornell in Hotel Management, Michelle had no problem getting approved for a $4,000,000 loan to purchase a very nice hotel.

The hotel that Michelle ended up buying was about five minutes from Downtown Atlanta and had annual net profits of over $600,000. The price of the hotel was $3.7 million and required Michelle to put down 25%, which was approximately $925,000 plus some costs to pay her broker in the transaction.

Although the income from her hotel was enough to live a very extravagant lifestyle, she maintained a very nice, modest living, only using revenue from the remaining apartment building.

She kept this up for three years accumulating over $2,000,000 in the bank. Of course not being one to settle for less, Michelle purchased a second hotel about 20 minutes from downtown. This time she stepped it up a little and made the purchase at $7,000,000. She put 25% down once again, which was approximately $1,750,000. This time it was well worth it as the hotel had annual net profits of almost $2.25 million.

With an income of approximately $3 million annually, she decided that it was time to sell her last apartment building, which she sold for a profit of $300,000. Life was great for Michelle and she went on to buy two more hotels within a three-year period and raised her total income to over $7 million annually. She also managed to grow her net worth to over $40 million before her 30th birthday.

Michelle is just one example of how someone can gain a life of riches in the world of real estate investing if he is focused and determined to provide a better life for himself and his family.

Real Estate Investing in All Climates

Unlike the stock market, great real estate investments can be found year round, no matter the economic season. During a downturn, trough, recovery, expansion, or peak, a great real estate investment can be found and profited from. Real estate can be a good investment no matter the season for several reasons, but there are two in particular that I would like to cover and are as follows.

1.) Foreclosures on Adjustable Rate Mortgages: Due to a never ending list of foreclosures, there are always underpriced homes on the market that must sell, in many cases, for approximately half of the appraised value. With the large use of ARMs (adjustable rate mortgages), more people than ever are falling victim to foreclosure as they can no longer make their mortgage payments once they adjust.

In many scenarios, such as when rates were extremely low and credit was easy to obtain, people took out 3/1 and 5/1 ARMs (please see "Chapter 4 – What You Need to Know About Mortgages" for details) with 4% interest rates. Not having good sight or vision for the future, they ignored the form at closing that stated that their interest rates could jump as high as 9.75% at the first adjustment period and another 1% annually until their interest rates reached a cap of 13%.

This, of course, made a very large difference when the payment adjusted and became almost twice as high as it was originally. In some cases, this causes the sellers to be put in a position to sell or be foreclosed upon; therefore, with the credit effects of a foreclosure being close to deadly, a credit savvy homeowner will do almost anything to avoid foreclosure.

This type of situation is always available for capitalization and is one of the main reasons why there are always good real estate investments around.

2.) **You Don't Have to Pay the Mortgage:** One of my favorite aspects of a good real estate investment is that the owner of the investment is rarely the one that ends up making the monthly mortgage payments. Generally, the mortgage and all other related expenses are paid by the tenants of the property by way of rents collected by the owner or the property management company on the behalf of the owner. So with real estate, it is common practice for the investor to borrow the money from the bank and let his or her tenants pay the money back while the investment grows in value.

So even in a situation where properties aren't appreciating at a fast pace, an investor can still enjoy the benefits of equity by way of timely monthly payments from the tenants; therefore, real estate is a good investment in all climates.

Spotting Good Investments

Spotting a good real estate investment can be a simple, yet challenging, task. Depending on a person's investment philosophy (everyone needs one), a good investment can be determined by many different things.

In my opinion, a property that has the potential to increase in value steadily over a three to five-year period as well as having a strong enough rental market in order for a tenant to cover all related expenses for the property is a good one. Of course it has to fit within each individual investor's investment goals, but generally this is enough for a property to get my time and attention.

To make sure a property meets these qualifications, it is important to do a cash flow analysis that adds all income from the property and subtracts all related expenses, which should include possible maintenance fees.

If after completing the required math your gut still tells you that the subject property may make a good one, it is a good idea to do more due diligence and look at the history of home sales in the area to see how fast they have been appreciating over the last three to five years.

When looking at these numbers, it is important to remember that home values generally increase a lot faster in markets of low interest rates and easy credit like we had in the early to mid-2000s as the demand for homes is a lot higher when mortgage interest rates are low and credit is easy to obtain.

As I said before, many things can make a good real estate investment depending on the philosophy of the investor as long as at the end of the day it makes a profit.

1031 Tax-Deferred Exchange

The 1031 tax-deferred exchange is one of the best ideas that the government ever came up with in regard to doing something helpful for real estate investors. If used properly, the 1031 exchange law can help a real estate investor become very rich in a much shorter time.

The 1031 tax-deferred exchange gives an investor the opportunity to sell a piece of property and put the total proceeds from the sale into another property without having to pay taxes on the gain or profit before doing so.

There are several stipulations/guidelines that must be adhered to in order to make this a success, and they are listed below.

1.) The properties must be a "like-kind" exchange. This means that the property sold and the new property that is being purchased must be similar to one another in reference to their character. For example, a home that was held for investment can only be exchanged for other real property that is for investment. This could mean a single-family home being traded for another single-family home or a single-family home being traded for a 20-unit apartment building. As long as the properties have like-kind character, the 1031 exchange can be applied.

2.) A new property must be identified within 45 days of the sale of the investment where the profits have come from.
3.) The trade or exchange must take place and close within 180 days of the sale of the investment where the profits have come from.
4.) The proceeds must be held at a qualified intermediary, such as a title company or bank that can act as an exchange bank. This means that you can't just deposit this money at your regular local bank without it acting as an exchange bank, and you definitely can't take the money home with you.
5.) The property must be held for a long enough period of time for it to appear that the intent of the acquisition was for investment and not just to immediately sell for a profit. Deciding if this requirement has been fulfilled is basically done on a case by case basis, but typically a year is sufficient.

To give you a clear illustration of how the 1031 tax-deferred exchange works, I'll give you the story of Jessica. Jessica had a Master of Science in Psychology, which she earned in less than two years after completing her four-year degree in business.

She had a lot on her side and she was determined to add wealth to the picture. She had a high paying job with a large oil company, but she was ready to live off of assets and spend her weekdays in the manner that she chose and work when she pleased.

After years of saving money, she purchased a small 10-unit apartment building for $300,000. Although she enjoyed the income that came in from the building on a monthly basis, she was ready to sell after two years as the property's value went from $300,000 to $525,000.

After selling the property, Jessica had net proceeds of $200,000, which she held at her local title company with the intention to purchase a like-kind property.

After two weeks (within the 45-day requirement), Jessica spotted a 20-unit apartment building that was selling for $750,000 and notified the title company that she had a property in mind.

After searching for another couple of weeks to see if she could find anything else that she wanted to invest the money in (the proceeds for a 1031 exchange can go into more than one property as long as they are all like-kind), she decided that she was going to put the entire $200,000 into her new building and closed within 75 days (within the 180-day requirement).

In this case, since Jessica used the 1031 exchange to perfection, she was able to avoid paying taxes on the $200,000 that she had gained from the sale of her original apartment building, which allowed her to put more money into a larger investment.

After holding this apartment building for three years, Jessica was again ready to sell as the value rose from $750,000 to $1.3 million. In this case, she was able to sell the property and gain a profit of over $550,000, which she again held at her local title company with the intention of buying a like-kind property.

This time around, she found two properties that she wanted to invest in. Being allowed to do so, she invested half of the money into an upscale 18-unit building and the other half into a large 30-unit apartment building.

One important thing to note when exchanging properties is that you do eventually have to pay taxes at the end of the line (if there ever is an end) when you finally sell a property and want to take some cash out and use in a different way other than to purchase a like-kind property.

Watching Jessica utilize her total profits to invest in like-kind properties should give a good picture of how it works and another idea on how you can make it a success for you.

Tax Benefits of Depreciation

Another great benefit with investing in real estate is the tax favor real estate investors receive. Although most homes, in healthy real estate markets, don't depreciate in value, a real estate investor is allowed to depreciate a residential investment property over 27.5 years (39 years for commercial property). This is a great benefit and usually makes most of the income received tax-free.

The way depreciation works is, it's considered an expense that is deducted from the income that's received. For example, if an investment property had $3,000 worth of net income and $3,000 worth of depreciation, the taxable income would be $0; therefore, no tax will be paid on the income from the property in this scenario.

The way depreciation is calculated is by dividing the purchase price (plus acquisition cost, such as legal fees and title insurance) of the investment property (minus the value of the land, as land can't be depreciated) by 27.5. For example, if an investment property (minus the land) costs $300,000, you would divide that by 27.5. That would give you $10,909 of depreciation that can be subtracted from the income for the property. If the net income is less than $10,909, the income received on this property would be basically tax-free.

This is a great benefit. The only slight downside is that this decreases your cost basis by the amount that it was depreciated by.

This means that it creates a larger profit at the time of sale, but if using the 1031 exchange, this downside is basically irrelevant.

Using Property Management Companies

A good property management company can be a real estate investor's best friend and, in some cases, can also be his worst enemy. A good property management company will fill any vacancies, collect all rents, mail your mortgage payments, perform any evictions (if necessary), and schedule any maintenance work that is required for the preservation of the property.

Just as a restaurant manager makes sure that everything is intact at his or her establishment, so does a good property management company.

A good property management company will do extensive credit and background checks before putting someone into your property and will be very firm, yet professional and respectful, about collecting rents on a timely basis.

A good property management company will save an investor from a million and one headaches, as the investor rarely, if ever, comes into contact or is introduced to the tenants. This means that at 3:00 a.m., if the hot water heater breaks down, instead of calling you, they will call the property manager. Also, if anything else is wrong or something needs to be taken care of, the property management company is where the buck stops as they won't even know you as the property owner.

Depending on the level of business you give a property management company, it will generally charge a management fee of 5 to 8 percent of the rents collected. It will also generally charge a fee for finding tenants that can range from a couple hundred dollars to as much as the first month's rent.

I find property management companies very useful, as I'm not a good landlord, nor do I ever want to be. One must be careful of unscrupulous property management companies that will steal from you, so it is important that your property manager send you a monthly statement and that you review it and question any discrepancies.

Flipping Real Estate

Although flipping real estate is probably considered more to be gambling than investing, I thought some of my readers would want me to cover it, so I'll touch on the basics of the matter.

Flipping real estate involves purchasing a property for a low price and then quickly reselling the property at a profit. Sometimes the property is assigned to a third party without the title ever being put into the investor's hands. Flipping can be done in many ways and I'll cover a couple to wrap up this chapter on real estate investing.

The two tactics that I'm going to cover are an outright purchase and then sell, and the other will be assigning a contract to a third party without ever taking possession of the property.

Purchase & Then Sell

This is probably the most common form of flip since many houses are rehabbed first before being put back on the market to be sold. This is almost impossible when assigning a contract and very risky as well. To give you a clear illustration of how this form of flipping would take place, I'll give you the story of Mya.

Mya was looking for some fast income and was informed about the possible benefits of flipping real estate from a casual friend of hers. Under his direction, she had some signs made with statements such as "We Buy Homes Fast" and "Avoid Foreclosure."

The first day the signs were up, she got about 15 calls. Not all of the calls were quality as many people wanted full value for their homes, which left no room to profit from for Mya if she bought a home at full price.

Eventually, Mya got a call from a desperate seller who had lost her employment with a prestigious accounting firm and needed to sell badly in order to avoid foreclosure. During the first two minutes of the phone call, Mya wisely found out that the home was worth $180,000, the lady owed $115,000, and she was willing to accept $125,000 for the property if Mya could purchase the home and close within 30 days.

Mya had excellent credit, so she was able to get financing and she purchased the property and closed within the 30-day time frame. The home was in a great area as it was located near some good schools and close to both shopping and highways.

Immediately, Mya had the interior painted and did some other minor work that in all cost her around $2,000. At this point, Mya had $127,000 invested in the home. She didn't have much of any closing costs when she bought the home because she agreed to a low closing costs loan that came with a much higher interest rate. This was a good idea as she was only going to be keeping this home for a short period of time.

After having the work done, Mya had the home appraised and it came back at $190,000. She then put ads in the newspaper stating that she had a $190,000 property selling for only $160,000.

Within hours after the ads were posted, she received numerous phone calls from motivated buyers who began bidding on the home, and the high demand allowed Mya to actually sell the home for $168,000. Remember supply & demand? The demand was higher than the supply. This gave Mya a quick profit of approximately $40,000, which she was very excited about. However, she was slightly disappointed when she learned that she would not be able to use the 1031 exchange since she held the property for inventory and not for investment.

This was just a simple example of flipping real estate after taking the title in your name and can be used by anyone with a little ambition to be a successful real estate flipper (not investor).

There are a couple potential downfalls with using this approach. Many mortgage lenders will not finance a home if the seller has not held title for a certain period of time. In some cases, the lender wants the title to be in the seller's name for a minimum of 60 days, and some may require 90 days. Not all mortgage companies have this requirement, but it is important to know exactly who you're doing business with and to make sure the buyer of the home is willing to use a lender that doesn't have a title seasoning requirement.

Another potential downfall could be the value of the property decreasing before the seller has had enough time to sell at a profit. This generally will not happen if you buy the home with a large enough gap (value of home versus what you paid for it), which was the case with Mya, but it can still happen depending on many things, including the neighborhood or the condition of the economy.

If you buy a home at the peak of a business cycle when inflation is skyrocketing, this will cause the Federal Reserve (Federal Open Market Committee) to raise interest rates (to control inflation), and property values will generally decline if unattractive interest rates appear on the market.

In some cases, if the demand for housing is much higher than the supply, high interest rates will not have as much of an effect on the value of homes since people still need a place to sleep.

Flipping real estate can be very lucrative if done correctly. It can also be very dangerous if done incorrectly, so be careful when choosing properties to flip.

Assigning Real Estate to a Third Party

Assigning real estate to a third party can either be an easy transaction, or on the flipside, can become a nightmare in hell, full of lawsuits and headaches.

For the most part, I like to consider people as being good hearted people who spend most of their time trying to be successful and don't really care about the next man or woman being successful as long as they are able to take care of their own basic needs.

Sometimes when flipping real estate, you learn that this is not always the case. Surprisingly, when some people find out that you are about to make a quick profit off of them, they look down at the situation.

Even if their needs are being met in the transaction, some people have a problem with yours being met as if you are supposed to do business so everyone else benefits except for you.

If you plan on assigning a real estate contract to someone, it is very important to notify everyone involved in writing from the beginning to help prevent any unnecessary lawsuits and legal headaches.

To now give you an illustration of flipping a property by assigning a contract, I'll give you the story of Kimberly.

One day while driving home from work, Kimberly noticed a "for sale" sign on a beautiful two story home. She didn't have a chance at a mortgage because her credit was in drastic need of repair, so she knew she couldn't flip the property by purchasing it outright as she couldn't get financing.

When she made the offer on the property, she listed the buyer of the home as herself or "assignee." She notified the seller that she was unlikely to be able to get approved for financing, which was a safe and ethical way out of the contract if needed.

Nevertheless, Kim was able to find a buyer that was willing to purchase the home for $10,000 more than Kim had it under contract for, which gave her a quick and easy $10,000 profit at closing.

Of course, Kim did the right thing and notified the new buyers immediately of what her plans were, and they were okay with it since they were able to get a home for 90% of its fair market value, which is the way it's supposed to be.

Last Words of Chapter

Following the techniques and knowledge found in this chapter will put you in position to live very comfortably if that is what you desire; at the very least, you will be prepared to go through the battles of purchasing your first home.

Buying a home can be a very mind boggling task when unprepared, so I hope you now feel that you can tackle this process with no problem. Also, if you never knew how to begin real estate investing, you should now know the basic steps to get started and possibly end up in a very good lifestyle supported by assets like Michelle.

Chapter 4

What You Need to Know About Mortgages

With all the talk about real estate investing, it is important to note that in most cases, without a mortgage, none of it would be possible. A mortgage is simply what you give the bank or lender for a loan for real property. The real property is generally the collateral for the loan.

In most cases, a person doesn't have the ability to buy a home or apartment building outright with cash; therefore, a loan is required to complete the transaction. Depending on the situation of the borrower, this may be an easy or difficult process.

A mortgage is definitely considered a secured loan, meaning that if the borrower defaults on the mortgage, the bank has the complete right and ability to repossess or foreclose on the home and then resell it in an attempt to get its money back.

Almost every bank provides mortgage loans since the demand for mortgages has dramatically increased over the last 20 years as more families have discovered the benefits of homeownership and have decided to purchase a home.

In the past, unless a person had 20% down, he or she was denied mortgage loans as the banks considered this borrower to be of high risk. This is a significant difference to the way mortgages are now given since practically anyone can now be qualified for a mortgage with little money down.

Things have definitely changed for the better for prospective homebuyers as they no longer have to jump through as many hoops to become homeowners.

Prime and Sub-Prime

The mortgage a person or family can usually qualify for is divided into two categories: prime and sub-prime. The difference between the two is usually tens or hundreds of thousands of dollars if both loans are held for the entire length of the loan.

The ideal situation of any potential homebuyer is to get his credit in order before buying a home so that he won't be faced with what some experts consider a predatory loan. However, many people will buy homes without getting their credit situation in good shape and, therefore, will be forced to accept less than decent interest rates on their mortgages.

A prime loan is for someone with good credit that usually meets all guidelines. In the past, prime loans were only given to people with credit scores in the 700s. This has dramatically changed as many programs now allow borrowers with credit scores in the 600s to qualify for prime loans.

A prime loan generally has a very good interest rate and very reasonable closing costs. Being in a position to qualify for a prime loan is the ideal situation as it will save a borrower a ton of money.

On the flipside of things, a sub-prime loan is for someone whose credit situation doesn't meet all guidelines and is generally just a "band-aid" loan, not intended to be held for the life of the loan.

A sub-prime loan may go to someone who is recently coming out of a bankruptcy, foreclosure, or someone who has a bad past of not paying credit related bills on time, and his credit score may be in the low 600s.

Generally, a sub-prime loan is meant to be kept for only two or three years as it is meant to be refinanced after the borrower has had time to improve his credit by paying his mortgage and other debts on time during that period.

It is important to note that many of the sub-prime lenders have gone bankrupt and many others have changed their guidelines to require better credit backgrounds than before the sub-prime housing crisis. If you have less than stellar credit, I would recommend seeking an F.H.A. loan, which comes with a great interest rate since F.H.A. loans are insured by the Federal Housing Administration.

Mortgages Based on Property Use

Not every mortgage is created equal as we will see throughout this chapter, and not every mortgage presents the same amount of risk to the lender. When a lender decides to loan money to someone, the main objective of the lender in the process is to find out how much risk the particular borrower presents to the potential lender.

A portion of the risk level is determined by the borrower's intentions for the subject property. There are generally three types of property: primary residence, second home, and investment property.

The way the lender or mortgage industry for that matter determines the level of risk associated to each one is by thinking which is the first to go? What this means is, the lender tries to use logic to figure out what type of property would be the first to go and have payments stopped being made on it if a person owned all three (primary, second home, and investment), and all income stopped coming in.

Investment Property

Of the three, an investment property is considered the first to go if all income stopped coming in and, therefore, carries the most risk and has the highest interest rate and closing costs. In 2011, a down payment of at least 15% is typical when financing an investment property.

An investment property also usually has tenants that hardly ever treat the home with the same care that the homeowner would, which adds an extra layer of risk that must be paid for by way of a higher interest rate and higher closing costs.

Although I don't recommend them, as they flirt with dishonesty, there are several ways that people try to get around paying this premium if buying an investment property. The most common thing that people have done over the last decade is list the home as a primary residence with the intention of moving into the home within 30 or 60 days after closing.

After moving into the home, with the exception of F.H.A. loans, some lenders have no minimum amount of time that you have to live there to satisfy the owner occupancy requirement before you retreat to a previously owned home or go off and buy a new one. However, it is important to note that many lenders have a one-year occupancy requirement. To give you a clear, ethical illustration of how this works, I'm going to give you the story of Monica. Before I begin with this scenario, I must warn you how important it is to be completely honest with your lender. Not being truthful with your lender is a very serious matter; therefore, be sure to find out the requirements of the lender that you are doing business with and be totally honest.

Monica was a business woman living in New Jersey and working in New York, who was the owner of two condos in New Jersey. Monica liked living in New Jersey, but she wanted to invest in a new condo that was being built near her place of employment in Lower Manhattan.

When she went online to get mortgage rates, she discovered that marking the home as an investment property versus a primary residence or second home would cost her an extra several thousand dollars and a 2% higher interest rate. She also noticed that it required a much larger down payment.

As she sat at the computer, she wondered how she could get the primary residence rate while still being honest about the situation. She was curious about how long she would have to stay in the home to fulfill the owner occupancy requirement, so she called the 800 number and spoke to one of the loan representatives.

He informed her that as long as she had the intent to move into the home and make it her primary residence within 30 days, it would be eligible for a primary residence rate and costs. He also informed her that after she moved into the home that there was no minimum on how long she had to remain a primary resident of that home.

She knew that this meant that she could move into the home for a year or less and then move out and back into one of her condos in New Jersey. Then she could turn it into an investment property by renting it out to a tenant while keeping her primary residence rate.

She took heed to this information and purchased the home as her primary residence. Instead of moving all of her things from New Jersey, she packed some of her clothes, bought a small amount of furniture, and submitted a change of address with the local post office. She lived at the home for about a year before renting it out and going back to her condo in New Jersey.

Second Home

A second home presents the second highest amount of risk and, therefore, has costs and interest rates that are higher than that of a primary residence but lower than that of an investment property. A second home is usually far away from a person's primary residence and may even be on a beach, such as a condo overseeing the waters in Miami.

Generally, there is not a big difference in pricing between a primary residence and a second home and, depending on the lender, pricing may be the same. However, in 2011, a down payment of at least 10% is typical with most lenders when financing a second home.

One thing a lender won't tolerate is a borrower purchasing a home 10 miles away from his current home and trying to label it as a second home. The mortgage company is going to automatically assume that this is going to be an investment property because of how close it is. The logic behind it is that, a reasonable person would not purchase a second home only a few minutes away from his primary residence since a second home is usually used for vacation or some type of getaway. If you are buying a property that you want listed as a second home, depending on the lender, it must be at least 120 miles away from your primary residence.

Primary Residence

A person's primary residence is considered the place where he intends to sleep, eat, and use the restroom on a consistent basis. As mentioned before, a home being purchased as a primary residence has the best rates and costs available to a potential borrower. Down payments on primary residences may be as low as 3% in some cases.

This is because a primary residence is considered to have the least amount of risk since a homeowner living in his own property is likely to oversee and take good care of the property. Also, if a person owned a primary residence, a second home, and an investment property and all income stopped coming in, the likely reaction of a reasonable person is to do all that he can to make payments on his primary residence as that is where he lives and shelters his family.

Criteria for Getting a Mortgage

If a person has done all the leg work to getting his credit situation in order, the mortgage qualifying process is generally full of choices more than limitations as someone with excellent credit, as stated before, can buy a home with as little as 3% down.

The mortgage qualifying process considers three things in order of importance: credit score, debt to income ratio (often referred to as DTI), and assets.

Credit Criterion

As told to me by one of my business professors in college, credit is the most important thing, so guard it with your life. Since the financial crisis, which played a key role in causing the Great Recession, many lenders have changed their guidelines to require much better credit than before. However, F.H.A. and VA loans are pretty easy to qualify for and allow financing to borrowers with credit scores in the 500s. Besides borrowers who are seeking F.H.A. or VA loans, a credit score in the mid to high 600s should qualify someone for conventional home financing. It is important, however, to not have any late payments on any credit accounts during the two-year period leading to your home purchase and to not have any open collection accounts.

Debt to Income (DTI) Criterion

The debt to income ratio, also known as DTI, is very important when applying for a mortgage. The debt to income ratio measures the level of debt of a borrower compared to his level of income. Most lenders in 2011 require debt to income ratios to be below 45%, but some are still underwriting loans for borrowers with debt to income ratios as high as 50% in some cases.

The DTI ratio of a person is calculated by adding up all of a person's debt as it appears in monthly payments on a person's credit report and dividing it by the gross monthly income of the borrower. To give you a clear example of how this works, I will give you the story of Jasmine.

Jasmine was looking to buy a home and had spent the last two years doing all that she could to get her credit in tip top shape. She knew that her credit was good but now had to figure out how much money she could afford to borrow for a conventional mortgage.

When she called her loan officer at the local bank, after seeing that she had great credit, he told her that he would need to calculate her DTI to figure how much of a home she could buy since the federal government, in 2010, banned all loans that were used before the credit crisis that didn't require adequate documentation. Now, all lenders must make a good faith determination, based on documented and verified information, that a borrower has the ability to repay the loan.

Because he's a salesman first and a loan consultant second, he invited her down to the bank so he could go over some things with her and ultimately sell her a loan since she had A-1 credit.

The loan officer told Jasmine that there were two ways to figure out her DTI and he wanted to share both ways with her for her own knowledge, which would then make his job easier as he wouldn't have to answer constant questions regarding the matter.

The first way was to add up all of her minimum monthly payments from debt listed on her credit report. On her credit report, she had a car loan that had a monthly payment of $250, three student loans totaling $200 a month, and a credit card with a $30 minimum payment. This put her total monthly debt at roughly $480 a month.

They assumed that Jasmine's mortgage payment, including taxes and insurance, would be roughly $1,200. This then put her total monthly debt at $1,680. Her gross monthly income from her employment was $3,500 on a $42,000 annual salary. To calculate her DTI, they divided the total monthly debt of $1,680 by her monthly gross income of $3,500 and calculated a debt to income ratio of 48% ($1,680/$3,500).

The loan officer told Jasmine that they needed to keep the DTI under 50% to make it through underwriting, so she shouldn't choose a home that has a higher monthly payment than the $1,200 they used to calculate her DTI. She understood, so of course she agreed, and then asked for him to show her the other way to calculate her DTI.

He told her that the other way didn't exactly calculate her DTI, but what it does is it assumes a certain DTI goal and then tells you the maximum monthly payment or total debt you can have to stay under that stated goal.

Jasmine was slightly confused, so he pulled out a clean piece of paper and started showing her the exact math formula he was speaking about. He told her that if she wanted to keep her DTI under 50%, she would take her gross monthly income, which was $3,500, and multiply it by .5.

He told her that the $1,750 represented the total amount of debt that she could have as far as minimum monthly payments in order to keep her DTI under 50% or .5. He then told her that she needed to subtract all current debt as shown on her credit report, which included her car payment of $250, her student loans of $200, and her credit card payment of $30.

After subtracting all of her debt from the $1,750 maximum figure, Jasmine was left with $1,270 that represented what could be spent on her new home's mortgage payment.

So, basically, what she did was take her monthly gross income of $3,500 and multiplied it by the desired debt to income ratio (in this case 50% or .5), which came out to $1,750. They then subtracted all of her current debt that was listed on her credit report from the $1,750 number. The amount that was remaining came out to be $1,270, which represented the amount that could be spent on a monthly mortgage payment while keeping her debt to income ratio under 50%.

As stated earlier, the debt to income ratio of a person is very important when applying for a mortgage loan and, just like your credit situation, must be intact and kept under certain limits to be approved.

Assets Criterion

Generally of all three, the assets section isn't as important since the guidelines are generally easy to meet for someone with a good income and savings history. Also, if a rational person (one who uses logic and valid reasoning) has been preparing to purchase a home, he would normally save up money for a down payment and closing costs.

When being qualified for a mortgage loan, the lender wants to make sure that you have the necessary funds to close, which generally include your down payment, closing costs, and several months of reserves. Reserves refer to money that will be remaining in your bank account or liquid investment accounts after closing.

Most lenders require at least three to six months of mortgage payments in reserves after closing. This is considered a security cushion in case the borrower has a glitch in employment or falls upon hard times.

In the case of such an event, the lender would hate for the borrower to default on the loan because he didn't have any savings and then have to foreclose on the property and try to sell it to get its money back.

Most lenders also require that the assets for closing, as well as any reserves, be "seasoned." This means that they want to see that the money has been there (in the account) or at least building for the last two to three months.

This is because, if given the opportunity, some people who don't have any reserves would just borrow money from a friend or family member and place it in their bank account so it shows on their statement and then take the money right back out and give it back to the person whom they borrowed it from, therefore, leaving the borrower with no reserves in actuality.

Types of Mortgages

When deciding on an actual mortgage product, a borrower has a lot of options to choose from based on what his needs are. Although there are possibly more mortgage products available than I care to know about, I will cover the most popular types with you, which include fixed and adjustable loans.

When deciding on a mortgage product, a person needs to have an idea of how long he plans on keeping the property, likely rate of appreciation in the area, and if his income will adjust throughout the length of the loan.

After a person successfully answers all of these questions, he should be able to pick the right mortgage product for himself that addresses his needs at the lowest cost possible. Here's a description of the most popular types of loans.

Fixed Rate Mortgage

A fixed rate mortgage is a mortgage where the interest rate and monthly payments stay the same for the duration of the loan. If a person plans on staying in a home for a long time or isn't sure about how long he will stay in a home, I would always recommend going with a fixed rate mortgage as it's always better to be safe than sorry.

The most popular fixed rates mortgages on the market are the 30-year fixed, 15-year fixed, 40-year fixed, and the 20-year fixed.

30-Year Fixed Mortgage

With a 30-year fixed mortgage, the amount borrowed is amortized (paid off) over 30 years. The interest at which the money is financed at stays the same (fixed) for the entire 30 years. During the 30-year period, the monthly mortgage payment stays the same, therefore, making it a fixed mortgage.

If the borrower makes extra payments toward the principal throughout the life of the loan, the monthly payment would still remain the same, and the only adjustment that would be made is to the number of payments that need to be made. This would of course shorten the life of the loan, all depending on how much extra is paid to the principal.

A 30-year fixed mortgage is generally more expensive than many of the other products, as the interest rate is fixed for 30 years, affording the borrower security from interest rate increases. Another reason for the higher cost is the ability to slowly pay back the loan over a 30-year period at the same low rate.

15-Year Fixed Mortgage

A 15-year fixed mortgage is amortized over 15 years and generally comes with a lower interest rate and lower closing costs than that of a 30-year fixed since you're paying the money back in half the time.

This mortgage is generally for someone who has enough income to afford the higher payments that would come with paying the mortgage off in half the time of a 30-year mortgage and someone who doesn't want to be tied to a mortgage for 30 years.

Although with a 15-year fixed mortgage you are paying the mortgage off in half the time of a 30-year fixed, the mortgage payment is only approximately a 30 to 40 percent increase, versus double, as many would think since you're cutting the length of the mortgage in half.

I actually like the 15-year fixed, especially for someone who can afford the slightly higher payments. I also like the fact of being able to own the property outright in 15 years, versus in 30 years, which can seem like a lifetime to some people.

40-Year Fixed Mortgage

The recent emergence of the 40-year fixed has allowed many families in certain areas of the country to afford homes when they otherwise would not be able to. As the name indicates, a 40-year fixed mortgage is amortized over 40 years and generally has higher closing costs and interest rates than a 30 and 15-year fixed since you're borrowing the money for a longer period of time.

The 40-year fixed has a lower payment of maybe 10 to 15 percent less than a 30-year fixed, which may sound small, but does wonders for many families living paycheck-to-paycheck.

Other fixed products are available, such as the 20-year and 10-year fixed, which are priced accordingly using the same logic that is used on pricing the other fixed products.

Adjustable Rate Mortgage

An adjustable rate mortgage is a mortgage which, after a certain period of time, the interest rate adjusts. This adjustment is usually upwards and is usually a large adjustment. The way lenders entice homebuyers to take a loan of this nature, knowing that the fixed product with a fixed interest rate is available, is by offering it with lower initial interest rates and closing costs.

Although this type of loan seems dangerous, it does have its perks and in some cases is the best option for someone buying a home and looking for a quality mortgage. A person who should want an ARM is someone who doesn't expect to be in the home long and plans to sell within a set period of time, say three, five, or seven years.

The interest rate tied to an ARM is usually fixed for a certain period of time and then adjusts, generally in accordance to an index, such as the LIBOR. Although the ARM is amortized over a 30-year period, if you plan on being in a home for a while, say at least 10 or 20 years, I recommend staying away from adjustable rate mortgages as they can increase your payment almost double in some scenarios, all depending on the position of the index when the mortgage is due to adjust.

The popularity of each ARM is hard to determine because it all depends on the specific needs and intentions of the borrower. For example, if I were planning on staying in a home for four to five years, I would consider a five-year ARM because it gives me a fixed interest rate for the entire time period that I plan on keeping the home.

A few ARM products, listed in order of length, are the 3/1 ARM, 5/1 ARM, and 7/1 ARM. The first number in the equation represents the number of years it is fixed for, and the 1 at the end of the equation represents how often it can adjust. For example, a 5/1 ARM has a fixed interest rate for the first five years and can adjust every one year after that.

3/1 ARM

A 3/1 ARM is a popular product for someone who expects to be in a home for three years or less. The interest rate on the 3/1 ARM is generally less than all other mortgage products since it only gives the borrower a three-year time frame of security where the interest rate is fixed before it adjusts.

The closing costs of a three-year loan are also generally less than most other mortgage products for the same reason as stated above. Anytime a person thinks he will be in the home for longer than three years, I wouldn't recommend a three-year ARM.

5/1 ARM

The 5/1 ARM is very similar to the 3/1 ARM as it is fixed for a certain period of time before it adjusts. It usually has a slightly higher interest rate than a 3/1 ARM as well as slightly higher closing costs since it gives two more years of security for the borrower. The more security you want from your mortgage loan, the more you will have to pay for it.

Interest-Only Mortgages

An interest-only mortgage provides a borrower with a lower monthly payment than that of a traditional mortgage that pays principal and interest. An interest-only mortgage is generally amortized over 30 years, but for a certain period of time, only interest payments are required.

For example, a 30-year fixed with a 10-year interest-only option would have a fixed interest rate for the entire 30 years, but only interest payments are due in the first 10 years. For the remaining 20 years of the mortgage, it would then basically turn into a 20-year fixed as the entire principal balance would then be amortized over the remaining 20 years of the loan.

Over the last decade or so, this product has become extremely popular in places like California and South Florida where property values have risen to unaffordable levels. This is just another example of the mortgage industry's attempt to increase profits and give everyone a chance at homeownership.

Interest-only loans generally have a higher interest rate and higher closing costs than a traditional principal and interest loan as the lender assumes more risk since the borrower isn't paying back any principal for a fixed period of time while the mortgage is in the interest-only stage.

Closing Costs

There are practically fees for closing with every mortgage loan. Even though some lenders will deceive you and tell you that they aren't charging you any closing costs for the loan, they are generally just hidden.

What I mean by hidden is that, if they are not charged to you up front at closing, they will generally be charged to you by way of a higher interest rate or with pre-payment penalties. It is important to note that pre-payment penalties have been banned when connected to sub-prime and adjustable rate mortgages.

Closing costs are fees associated with the lender providing you with the loan. Lenders will sometimes break the fee down into countless items, which I think is more confusing than anything, and some will just charge you one up-front fee for the loan.

When companies decide to break these fees down, they generally list them as origination, processing, underwriting, discount points (if any), application fee, and several other junk fees. I don't like this idea as what matters to me is the total fee that the lender is charging me for the loan.

I have no care (and you shouldn't either) to know exactly what department my money is going to because once it's in the lender's hands, it can't be of any benefit to me, therefore, leaving me without a reason to care about how the company is going to be dividing the money.

What matters to me is the total fee that I'm paying for the loan to the lender. This is very similar to how many other regular businesses operate. For example, McDonald's doesn't give a breakdown of how the cost of the Big Mac added up to $3.49. Even if McDonald's did offer a breakdown, there's no reason to want it as the only thing that should matter is the total cost that you are paying for the sandwich.

On top of the fees that the lender charges for the loan, other closing costs would include what are called third parties, which are the appraisal, title insurance, and closing attorney's fees. These fees usually add up to about $1,500 to $2,500 depending on the size and value of the house.

In some states, there are also government and transfer taxes that must be paid at closing, but similar to the third party fees, these are not charges from the lender and will have to be paid no matter what lender you use.

Because closing costs also include third party fees, when the lender fees are broken into 15 different fees, they can be confused as third parties and vice versa. A good way to measure the total lender fees that you are paying from one lender to the next for a loan is to compare the APRs for the same interest rate.

The APR for a mortgage is described as the total cost of the loan put into an annual percentage rate. What this does is, it takes the interest rate and adds in the closing costs to come up with a percentage rate that you are actually paying for the loan over the entire duration of the loan.

This is a good way to compare one lender to another. For example, if both companies are offering a 30-year fixed with an interest rate of 6.25%, but the APR for one of the companies is 6.5% versus 6.78% for the other, this would let you know that the company with the higher APR is the one that is charging you the most in lender fees, which is what's important as your third party closing costs and taxes are going to be the same with any lender that you use even if you are told otherwise.

In an attempt to make you think that they have the lower fees, some lenders will sometimes give low-ball estimates on your third party closing costs to make your total closing costs look less than they really are. This is very deceitful. The way to overcome falling victim to this is to compare the APR between each mortgage company that you are considering doing business with.

Private Mortgage Insurance

Private mortgage insurance, also known as PMI, is required for borrowers that don't have at least 20% down. The borrower pays for the policy that covers the lender in case the borrower defaults on the loan.

Generally, the borrower gets no benefit from paying private mortgage insurance as the lender is the only one who benefits from it in case the borrower defaults on the loan and the lender is forced to foreclose and sell the property to try to get its investment back.

Where the lender benefits from the private mortgage insurance is, depending on the policy that it has, if it needs to foreclose on the property and sell it, the difference between what it sells the home for and the remaining balance left on the mortgage is made up by the insurance company that underwrote the private mortgage insurance policy.

Once the loan-to-value ratio is 80% or less, the borrower no longer has to pay private mortgage insurance and it falls off of the monthly payment. There are generally two ways to get the PMI taken off. If the mortgage balance goes down to 80% of the original home value at the time of purchase, the lender will automatically drop the PMI from your monthly payment since it is required to do so by law.

The second way to get PMI off of your monthly payment applies if your home appreciates in value so that you now have 20% of equity in the home. If this is the case, you must call the lender and pay to have a licensed appraiser come out and appraise the home. If it finds out that the home has appreciated to a point where it gives you 20% of equity, the lender will promptly remove the PMI from your mortgage payment. It is important to note that F.H.A. borrowers will have to pay PMI for a minimum of five years and until their loan-to-value reaches 78%, which is the equivalent to having an equity interest of 22% in the home.

PMI is very undesirable. A way to get above 80% financing without having to pay PMI is to get an 80/10 piggy back loan. With an 80/10 loan, you get two separate loans, one for 80% of the mortgage and another for the remaining 10% of the mortgage.

The second mortgage that is for the smaller amount generally has a much higher interest rate than the first mortgage. It is riskier for a lender to have the second position on the home in case of default as it is normally with a totally different lender than the first mortgage.

Even though the interest rate on the second mortgage is generally a lot higher than that of the first, the monthly payment generally still comes out cheaper than doing the one loan that has PMI.

Refinancing

Refinancing a mortgage means getting a new loan on a home that you already own and have a mortgage on or at some point had a mortgage on if it has been paid off. There are two main reasons for a person to refinance a loan: a rate and term adjustment or to get cash out.

Rate and Term Refinance

There are generally two situations when a person would do a rate and term refinance. The first reason is if he has an adjustable rate mortgage that has adjusted or is about to adjust and the borrower wants to lock in a lower fixed interest rate for the remainder of the loan.

The second reason for someone to do a rate and term refinance is if he locked in an interest rate when rates were relatively high and interest rates have come down to where refinancing is a great option in order to lock in a lower payment.

Cash-Out Refinancing

There's generally only one reason to do a cash-out refinance and that is to get some cash out. The reasons why you may want to get the cash out are plenty and may include doing some home improvements, to bail your husband or wife out of jail, or to pay off credit cards.

Generally, when doing a cash-out refinance, some lenders will allow a borrower to raise the loan amount to between 85 and 95 percent of the value of the home; however, with the current credit crisis, many lenders are only underwriting much lower loan-to-value refinances.

When doing a refinance, both rate and term and cash-out, it's important to know that you have a three-day rescission period after closing and signing all the paperwork to cancel and back out of the loan. The three-day period includes Saturdays, but not Sundays and holidays.

If for any reason after closing on a refinance you feel uncomfortable with the new loan that you've selected, you can back out within three days with no penalty.

Last Words of Chapter

Knowing the basics of any business will allow you to operate within that world and at the least give you what you need to be able to oversee a transaction to know what's going on or to see if someone is getting played or not, which is very important as it may be you who's the one getting played.

Mortgage information is also very valuable as you will need one to invest in one of the best investments in the world. It is also good to know your mortgage options since picking the right mortgage for your situation might determine if the investment you make is going to be profitable or not.

Chapter 5

Accounting for Investors

When it comes to investing, there are certain accounting basics which must be known and understood very well in order to prevent your investing efforts from becoming gambling, which is the true title for the action that is done when someone without the proper information attempts to invest.

This chapter isn't going to be about traditional accounting that would include talks about inventory and similar topics. This chapter is more about the accounting information needed to make intelligent investment decisions.

From time to time you hear people talking about how certain companies have great stocks or how they are "must-buys." Then when you ask them how much cash the company has on hand they become dumbfounded. If you then ask what are its quarterly liabilities compared to its cash on hand or quarterly income, they may look at you even crazier. Most amateur investors invest on advice that they've received without performing their own due diligence.

To reduce the chances of buying a bad investment, one must be educated on the particulars of what makes a company healthy from a financial point of view. If you knew that a company had quarterly debt obligations of $2 billion and quarterly income of only $1.2 billion on average over the last few years, one might be a little more skeptical about becoming a shareholder.

This company is obviously losing money on a regular basis. Once that happens, it's not too long before talks of bankruptcy emerge, and after that, you can be sure of a declining stock price.

Before investing, it is important to learn where to find such vital information and how to determine if it's good or bad from an investment point of view. This important information is open to the public for all publicly traded companies and can be found on the Yahoo! Finance page after entering the company's ticker symbol in for a stock quote.

In my opinion, the two most important sources of information are the balance sheet and the income statement. These two items basically tell an investor everything that is needed to know about the financials of a company. Their importance can be considered similar to checking the blood pressure or sugar level of a diabetic. In some situations, after looking at a company's balance sheet or income statement, you may be warned that the company needs some immediate medical attention as it may be dying slowly.

Balance Sheet

The balance sheet can be described as an X-ray of the financial condition of the company. It is divided into three sections: assets, liabilities, and stockholders' equity. The assets section shows how much cash the company has on hand, value of any investments, value of all accounts receivable (money owed to the company), and value of all other assets.

The liabilities section shows everything that the company owes. This will include all accounts payable, long-term debt, and any other dollar amount that the company owed someone at the time of the X-ray. This section is very important and, combined with the assets section, lets you know if the company has enough money to pay its bills if all revenues stopped coming in (which is unlikely with most large companies).

The stockholders' equity section shows the amount of ownership the shareholders as a whole have in the company, which is the result of the amount of assets subtracted by liabilities. In my opinion, the stockholders' equity portion isn't as important as the first two sections but does include such items as treasury stock (company stock that the company has in its treasury) and retained earnings (all money kept by the company after paying dividends).

Carefully looking at a company's balance sheet can stop someone from making a very bad investment decision since knowing how much cash a company has versus the amount of its short-term debt obligations can be the deciding factor of success or failure, especially when investing in a small cap company. The next page shows a recent copy of Walmart's balance sheet.

Period Ending	Oct 31, 2010	Jul 31, 2010	Apr 30, 2010	Jan 31, 2010
	Assets			
	Current Assets			
Cash And Cash Equivalents	10,616,000	10,195,000	8,516,000	7,907,000
Short Term Investments	-	-	-	-
Net Receivables	4,374,000	4,531,000	4,235,000	4,144,000
Inventory	41,059,000	34,793,000	35,503,000	33,160,000
Other Current Assets	3,519,000	3,526,000	3,420,000	3,120,000
Total Current Assets	**59,568,000**	**53,045,000**	**51,674,000**	**48,331,000**
Long Term Investments	-	-	-	-
Property Plant and Equipment	106,542,000	103,814,000	102,928,000	102,307,000
Goodwill	16,586,000	15,993,000	15,859,000	16,126,000
Intangible Assets	-	-	-	-
Accumulated Amortization	-	-	-	-
Other Assets	4,194,000	4,092,000	3,910,000	3,942,000
Deferred Long Term Asset Charges	-	-	-	-
Total Assets	**186,890,000**	**176,944,000**	**174,371,000**	**170,706,000**
	Liabilities			
	Current Liabilities			
Accounts Payable	55,435,000	55,049,000	53,261,000	50,550,000
Short/Current Long Term Debt	12,895,000	10,531,000	11,177,000	4,919,000
Other Current Liabilities	77,000	75,000	74,000	92,000
Total Current Liabilities	**68,407,000**	**65,655,000**	**64,512,000**	**55,561,000**
Long Term Debt	43,899,000	38,702,000	35,780,000	36,401,000
Other Liabilities	-	-	-	-
Deferred Long Term Liability Charges	6,197,000	5,368,000	5,152,000	5,508,000
Minority Interest	2,495,000	2,250,000	2,273,000	2,180,000
Negative Goodwill	-	-	-	-
Total Liabilities	**120,998,000**	**111,975,000**	**107,717,000**	**99,650,000**
	Stockholders' Equity			
Misc Stocks Options Warrants	367,000	323,000	325,000	307,000
Redeemable Preferred Stock	-	-	-	-
Preferred Stock	-	-	-	-
Common Stock	3,969,000	3,999,000	4,059,000	378.000
Retained Earnings	61,451,000	61,746,000	62,486,000	66,638,000
Treasury Stock	-	-	-	-
Capital Surplus	-	-	-	3,803,000
Other Stockholder Equity	105,000	(1,099,000)	(216,000)	(70,000)
Total Stockholder Equity	**65,525,000**	**64,646,000**	**66,329,000**	**70,749,000**
Net Tangible Assets	**$48,939,000**	**$48,653,000**	**$50,470,000**	**$54,623,000**

Income Statements

As equally important as the balance sheet is the income statement. The income statement has two very simple, but important, sections: revenues and expenses. The revenue section shows all income that the company had come in during the period and the cost of that revenue (also known as cost of goods sold). The difference between the two is the gross profit or margin. High margins are good, but a margin that is too high may indicate a product that is priced inappropriately.

The expense section, on the other hand, has all expenses that the company incurred during the period, such as rent, payroll, research fees, and all other items grouped in sections that cost the company money during the period.

The difference between the income section and the expense section is the net profit (or loss). The larger the profit, generally, the better for stock prices, and when push comes to shove, is the real reason a company's stock price either appreciates or declines. The numbers derived from the income statement are the numbers used to calculate the company's earnings per share (EPS) and price to earnings ratio (P/E).

It is important to educate yourself in these areas and become a seasoned investor and not someone who takes advice from a financial advisor without doing any of his own due diligence. The next page shows a copy of a recent Walmart income statement.

Period Ending	Oct 31, 2010	Jul 31, 2010	Apr 30, 2010	Jan 31, 2010
Total Revenue	**101,952,000**	**103,689,000**	**99,848,000**	**113,751,000**
Cost of Revenue	75,906,000	77,520,000	74,703,000	85,291,000
Gross Profit	**26,046,000**	**26,169,000**	**25,145,000**	**28,460,000**
Operating Expenses				
Research Development	-	-	-	-
Selling General and Administrative	20,435,000	20,014,000	19,373,000	21,054,000
Non Recurring	-	-	-	-
Others	-	-	-	-
Total Operating Expenses	-	-	-	-
Operating Income or Loss	**5,611,000**	**6,155,000**	**5,772,000**	**7,406,000**
Income from Continuing Operations				
Total Other Income/Expenses Net	53,000	57,000	51,000	53,000
Earnings Before Interest And Taxes	5,664,000	6,212,000	5,823,000	7,459,000
Interest Expense	569,000	542,000	522,000	522,000
Income Before Tax	5,095,000	5,670,000	5,301,000	6,937,000
Income Tax Expense	1,505,000	1,946,000	1,834,000	1,982,000
Minority Interest	(154,000)	(151,000)	(143,000)	(175,000)
Net Income From Continuing Ops	3,590,000	3,724,000	3,467,000	4,955,000
Non-recurring Events				
Discontinued Operations	-	-	-	(57,000)
Extraordinary Items	-	-	-	-
Effect Of Accounting Changes	-	-	-	-
Other Items	-	-	-	-
Net Income	**3,436,000**	**3,573,000**	**3,324,000**	**4,723,000**
Preferred Stock And Other Adjustments	-	-	-	-
Net Income Applicable To Common Shares	**$3,436,000**	**$3,573,000**	**$3,324,000**	**$4,723,000**

Types of Income

It's important to know that there are three different types of income and that they get treated differently for tax purposes. It sounds crazy, but the income which requires sweat and blood is taxed heavier than income that is received without lifting a finger. It sounds backwards. However, instead of fighting with it,

I recommend adjusting your game plan so the laws become in your favor. The three different types of income are earned income, passive income, and portfolio income.

Earned Income

Earned income is the most commonly received income. When working on a job, the income that is received is considered earned income as it was worked for and, therefore, earned. Earned income is taxed at the highest rates.

Passive Income

Passive income is income that is received without any or much work being done by the investor. Income from having an ownership interest in a limited partnership would be considered passive income, as well as income received from real estate. Passive income is taxed the same way as earned income, except that most real estate income will be tax-free due to the multiple tax deductions involved in having investment real estate.

I would much rather prefer to have passive income versus earned income as it symbolizes that I am receiving income without lifting a finger. As with earned income, people can only get it from one place at a time since they can only be in one place at a time. With passive income, because it generally doesn't require the investor's presence, it can be received from multiple places at once.

Portfolio Income

Portfolio income is income that is received from having ownership in paper assets, such as stocks, bonds, and mutual funds. Dividends from stocks and interest from bonds are examples of portfolio income. Portfolio income is generally taxed at much lower rates than earned and passive income; therefore, portfolio income is very attractive. This is another form of income that doesn't need to be worked for.

Capital Gains & Losses

Stocks and bonds are considered capital assets. If a capital asset is sold for more than it was paid for, it is recognized as a capital gain. On the other hand, if a capital asset is sold for less than it was paid for, then it is considered a capital loss. If the capital asset is held for a minimum of one year before it is sold at a profit, then it would be considered a long-term gain.

The good thing about long-term capital gains is that they are taxed at a maximum rate of 15%. Dividends paid on stocks held for more than 60 days are also taxed at a maximum of 15%.

Last Words of Chapter

The accounting basics that were discussed in this chapter are only a small fraction of accounting concepts. However, they are the important basics needed to invest wisely in your mission to becoming financially free.

From reading and carefully analyzing a company's income statement to making investment decisions with the tax rate of different forms of income in mind, this chapter is very important and needs to be understood very well if someone is going to consider becoming an active investor.

Chapter 6

Investing in Stocks

Although stocks may have looked bad in the comparison to real estate, stocks can be a very good investment if used with the right game plan. I do not, however, believe that a person's investments should be in all stocks, just as I don't believe a person's dinner should be made up of all side items.

Like I mentioned earlier, stocks can be a great investment if used properly; throughout this chapter, I will be teaching you how to use them properly to maximize profits while minimizing the potential for losses at the same time.

What Are They?

Stock, which is also used interchangeably with the word *share*, represents an ownership interest in a corporation. So it can be said that if you are a shareholder of a particular company, say Home Depot or Nike for instance, then you are part owner of that company. Stocks can be divided between common stock and preferred stock. Most of the time when investing in equities, it will be in common stock. Not all companies issue preferred stock, although it does provide a shareholder with certain distinct benefits.

Owners of preferred stock get paid dividends before those of common stock, and if the company goes bankrupt, they would get money before owners of common stock. On the downside, only owners of common stock are eligible to vote on issues that require shareholder approval.

Generally, only small amounts of preferred stock get issued as common stock is what's most common as it gives you real ownership powers such as voting on mergers or who should be on the board of directors.

When a business decides to incorporate (which will be discussed in a later chapter) its operation into a corporation, the company gets authorized to issue a certain number of shares, which is equivalent to selling pieces of ownership in the business.

Shares of a business can be compared to cutting a pie into many pieces. The more pieces of the pie you own, the more of the company you own also. Incorporating a business and issuing (selling) shares is just like dividing the ownership of a business into many pieces, and whoever holds the most pieces, individually or collectively, has the most control over the company.

Just like any other business, the shareholders of most major companies get their fair share of profits when they are distributed by way of dividends (will be covered later in this chapter).

Being a shareholder definitely has its privileges besides sharing in profit, as the more you own, the more control you have over that company. Shareholders are responsible for voting for the board of directors who oversee the company and hire top company positions, such as the president and chief executive officer.

Shareholders have the right to attend shareholder annual meetings where they can participate in voting on company issues, such as if the company should merge and become partners with another entity.

This means that if you are able to get a large enough share of the company, you could heavily influence the direction of the company and maybe even place yourself into an executive position, but that all depends on if you own a large enough piece of the pie to vote yourself in.

Most large companies that we buy our everyday products from, such as Walmart, Home Depot, McDonald's, and Target are considered public companies and have shares that are available for purchase by the general public.

This gives any and everybody, from the President of the United States to the janitor in charge of changing light bulbs at the local hospital, a chance to own a piece of the largest companies in the world. Each company has its own ticker symbol that's used when buying and selling stocks on the stock market. For example, Walmart's ticker symbol is "wmt," and Ford's ticker symbol is "f."

Classification of Stocks

Stocks are often classified based on the type of company it is, the company's value, or in some cases, the level of return that is expected from the company. Some companies grow faster than others, while some have reached what they perceive as their peak and don't think they can handle more growth. In some cases, management just might be content with the level of business that they've achieved and, therefore, may stall to make moves to increase market share.

Before investing in a particular company, it is very important to get to know the company on a personal level and find out what the company's goals and objectives are for the short and long-term. Some companies are growth minded, while some are defensive minded and operate in services that are always needed, such as food.

In order to prosper in the world of stock investing, a person must have a clear understanding of what he is doing or he shouldn't be doing it at all. Investing in stocks can be very risky, all depending on the level of knowledge held by the person making the investment decisions. Below is a list of classifications that are important to know.

Blue Chip Stocks

Blue chip stocks represent the largest companies in the world, such as Walmart, American Express, and Home Depot. These companies usually have very high earnings year after year and have a reputation of stability and exceptional corporate management.

These companies have great financial strength and often share the profits of the business on a quarterly basis with their shareholders. These companies aren't as concerned with growth because due to their business model, with the birth of every child, more business is automatic for a lot of these companies.

Because of the financial strength of most blue chips, they generally make for good investments despite the business cycle as long as the company that you are investing in shares your personal goals and objectives. If you are looking to invest in a company that will grow at a rapid pace and a company tells you that it is maintaining its current size as it can't handle more business right now, then this is not the company for you as it doesn't share your current objectives.

Growth Stocks

Growth stocks represent companies whose sales and profits are growing faster than the average company within their individual sector or industry. These companies are usually very aggressive and are actively acquiring other companies to help them achieve their growth goals. These companies usually have very aggressive marketing plans and focus heavily on branding their names, which ultimately gets their products inside of our homes.

Growth stocks usually don't pay dividends to shareholders during the growth stages of the company as they retain the majority of company profits to grow the company with, which can often mean acquiring (buying) other companies.

So, as I said before, if you are considering investing in stocks, get to know the company on a personal level because the company's goals may be the exact opposite of your personal investment goals. If you are looking for a company that will pay you dividends (company profits) every quarter, then a growth stock is not what you are looking for.

Defensive Stocks

Defensive stocks are companies that are generally stable in all economic climates as they are companies that provide important goods and services that are used in good as well as bad economic times. These would include shares of electric companies, food suppliers, tobacco companies, and beverage companies like Coca-Cola.

These companies will usually hold their own (market position) in the worst of economic times, such as a downturn or recession, therefore, making defensive stocks good investments during business cycles where other investments are plunging or declining rapidly in value.

Income Stocks

Income stocks are generally some of my favorite stocks as they offer above average dividend (profit) payments to their shareholders.

These companies are usually very stable and have gained a large market share and can afford to heavily reward their shareholders.

Income stocks are usually very attractive to retired people who depend on the consistent dividend payments every quarter. These are companies that are usually comfortable and content with their current market position and have focused on maintaining their current business. This is not always the case, but generally it is.

Cyclical Stocks

Cyclical stocks are stocks of companies whose sales and profits generally fluctuate (move up and down) depending on the business cycle or condition of the economy. For example, during bad economic times, cyclical stock prices decline, and in good economic times, their earnings and stock prices generally increase.

Although cyclical stocks can be used to maximize profits in recovering and expanding economic times, I'm not a fan of high volatility. In times of prolonging economic hardship, the stock prices of these companies generally continue to decrease, and sometimes these companies even fall into bankruptcy and lose their market position altogether.

Large Cap Stocks

Large cap stocks are generally blue chip companies that are powerhouse businesses and have a large piece of the market share. This is not always the case as some large cap companies have negative earnings and declining sales.

This is possible because unlike blue chip companies that get their name from being stable and proven companies, a large cap company is just a company with market capitalization of over

$10 billion. The market capitalization of a company is determined by multiplying the company's stock price by the number of shares outstanding.

During the period right before the tech stock bubble burst is a good example of when many companies didn't make any profits, but because of an inflated stock price, were labeled as large cap companies. On the other hand, you earn the title of being a blue chip company with long-term sales and profits.

Mid Cap Stocks

A mid cap company is a company with a market capitalization of greater than $2 billion, but less than $10 billion. Generally, a mid cap company will not pay any dividends as it is using all of the company's profits to grow and expand its current level of business. This is usually okay with its shareholders since they invested for growth and not for dividends unless they invested without knowing what they invested in.

Small Cap Stocks

Small cap stocks are stocks of companies that have less than $2 billion in market capitalization. These are usually growing companies with very aggressive marketing plans as they are in a position to either sink or swim.

Small cap companies rarely ever pay any dividends as they generally need every dollar that they can get to help either expand the business or, in many scenarios, to stay afloat. Many small cap companies go out of business before making it out of the small cap category, which makes this a very critical stage in the life of the business.

No matter what your goals are, it is very important to know exactly what business cycle you are in and the detailed business profile of the company that you are considering investing in. It is very important to know exactly what you are doing before you start doing it.

Private Equity

A lot of money can be made investing in private equities. Private equities are companies that are not listed on any public exchange. These companies are usually pretty small and, therefore, offer a lot of upside and are, for the most part, only available to accredited investors since they are considered very risky. Accredited investors include individuals with a net worth exceeding $1 million. Annual income of $200,000 for an individual or joint income of $300,000 for a married couple also qualifies the individual(s) as accredited. Investment firms and banks are other examples of accredited investors. Berkshire Hathaway, led by Warren Buffett, is an example of a company that has successfully invested in private equities.

Mutual Funds

With all the talk of the need for diversification in today's marketplace, a lot of people are turning to mutual funds. A mutual fund is a collection of companies from different sectors, industries, market caps, and often countries that make up one share.

If a person buys one share of a mutual fund, he would potentially own a piece of approximately 100 companies. To some people this is considered diversification as they own a piece of many companies instead of just one or a few.

For the record, I believe diversification is being in several totally different investments. For example, owning two hotels, a book publishing company, a clothing line, and shares of Coca-Cola and Exxon Mobil would symbolize diversification to me. It doesn't have to be in these specifics businesses or stocks, but hopefully you get the picture.

In regards to having a diversified portfolio, my opinion on mutual funds is that they are for amateur investors who don't know how to pick their own investments or for experienced investors who, for one reason or another, don't have the time to. Although mutual funds can give a person professional management of investments, the downside to that is that mutual fund companies generally charge large fees that eat a large portion of the profits on a continual basis. I'm not at all a fan of this, especially when the mutual fund company doesn't assume any of the risk.

On the upside, there are mutual funds which are tied to indexes such as the S&P 500 (measure of the stock performance of 500 of the largest companies) that have much smaller fees than traditional mutual funds as less work and research are performed since they are just tied to the index.

Depending on the investment skill level of the individual, mutual funds may need to play a vital role in a person's investment portfolio in order to give him some level of diversification that he would normally not otherwise have if making all investment decisions on his own.

Hedge Funds

Hedge funds, which are lightly regulated, are very popular investment vehicles that are limited to wealthy and sophisticated investors. The first hedge fund was created in 1949 by Alfred Jones, who believed in having long positions on assets that he expected to outperform the general market and selling short assets that he expected would underperform the general market. Such a strategy was seen as a hedge to the risks inherent in the market; therefore, the term hedge fund was created.

Although not always, the typical hedge fund is formed as a limited liability partnership. The investors are the limited partners and the general partner is usually the investment manager, which is often a separate company that has been hired by the hedge fund. The best hedge funds have been known to dramatically outperform the general market with respect to returns.

Hedge funds usually have a 2/20 fee structure, which pays the investment manager an annual 2% management fee of the net asset value of the fund and a 20% bonus, also called performance fee, of the annual return. Such payments are often paid monthly or quarterly. All of the fund's expenses are usually taken from the 2% management fee.

Hedge funds employ a variety of strategies with the most common funds having long and short positions in equities. Some, however, have mixed strategies where many different investment strategies are employed. Many hedge funds are highly leveraged, which means that they will often borrow money or trade on margin, which allows the fund to invest with assets that far outweigh the assets that actually belong to the fund. This can dramatically increase the return that a fund can achieve, while also increasing the level of risk. However, many fund managers will apply the least amount of leverage to the riskiest assets and the most amount of leverage to investments with the least amount of risk, such as U.S. bonds. There are several terms with relation to hedge funds that should be understood.

Hurdle Rates

A hurdle rate is not used in many funds; however, funds with hurdle rates require the fund to achieve a certain return before the fund pays the investment manager a performance fee. Hurdle rates are usually small and may range from 4 to 6 percent and no performance fee may be paid until the fund reaches the set rate. For example, a fund with a hurdle rate of 5% will not pay a performance fee to the fund's manager until the fund surpasses a 5% return. The exact details of the hurdle rate requirement will often be articulated in the partnership agreement.

High Water Marks

High water marks prevent investment managers from being paid on the same returns twice. When a fund has a decrease in net asset value, the fund manager will not be paid a performance fee until the net asset value surpasses the previous peak in net asset value which was used to pay a prior performance fee. For example, if a fund paid a performance fee when the fund had a net asset value of $10 million, and then the fund's net asset value decreases to $9 million, the fund would not be obligated to pay a performance fee until the fund's net asset value surpasses the $10 million mark. The return from $9 million in net asset value to $10 million would not be considered a basis for a performance fee because of the high water mark provision. I recommend not investing in any hedge fund that doesn't have a high water mark provision.

Surrender fees

Surrender fees, which are also commonly known as redemption or withdrawal fees, charge investors a set percentage for withdrawing money from the fund. The terms for surrender fees may vary; however, most funds will typically only charge surrender fees for withdrawals that occur within a certain period of time or for withdrawals that occur outside of acceptable withdrawal periods. In many cases, the surrender fee is returned to the fund and benefits the remaining investors. Sometimes, however, the surrender fee is retained by the investment manager for his benefit.

Short-Selling

Short-selling is a great way to profit from equities in a falling market. Short-selling involves an investor borrowing securities, usually from a broker, and selling them. This transaction is based on the assumption that the underlying security will decrease in value, which will allow the investor to repurchase the securities at a later date (at a lower price) and return them to the broker. Without regard to fees that must be paid to the broker for borrowing such shares, the difference between what the shares are initially sold for and what they are repurchased for is the profit (or loss) for the investor.

Short-selling can be very dangerous in a rising market. Even in a declining market, there is a substantial amount of risk involved when short-selling. After going short on an equity, if it rises in value, the investor would be required to repurchase the shares at a much higher cost than what he was able to sell them for initially. Without owning an equal amount of the shares that are sold short, one way to limit the risk that is inherent with short-selling is to buy a call option on the same stock; therefore, if the stock has an unexpected increase in price, the investor would be covered since he has the option to purchase the stock at a price that is either the same, slightly lower, or slightly higher than the price the shares were at when they were initially sold by the investor.

Margin Trading

Margin trading is a good way to increase your rate of return if you are an astute investor; however, margin trading also has substantial risks that can quickly deplete an account if the wrong investments are purchased on margin. Margin trading involves borrowing money, with interest being charged, from your brokerage firm to purchase stocks, which become collateral that the brokerage firm can sell without any notice to you to cover a margin call. FINRA (Financial Industry Regulatory Authority) requires that investors with margin accounts maintain a minimum of 25% in equity of the total market value of all securities in the margin account. Some firms, however, have larger maintenance requirements than the legally required 25%. If an investor's equity goes below the required maintenance level, a margin call will generally be placed for the investor to deposit more money or to sell shares to bring the account in compliance.

By law, a brokerage firm is required to obtain an investor's signature before allowing him to trade on margin. Also, by law, an investor is required to deposit at least $2,000 with his brokerage firm before being allowed to trade on margin. Although some brokerage firms allow less to be borrowed, Regulation T of the Federal Reserve Board allows an investor to borrow up to 50% of the price of securities.

Exchange Markets

Just like the farmers in the first chapter, stock investors need a place to trade and exchange their stocks; therefore, exchange markets were created. There are many exchange markets, but only two exist that I feel the need to cover. The exchange markets which

I'm going to cover in order of popularity are the New York Stock Exchange (NYSE) and NASDAQ.

New York Stock Exchange

The New York Stock Exchange (NYSE) was created in 1792 and is the largest exchange for stocks (equities) in the world. It is commonly referred to as the "Big Board" as it is the home to many of the largest companies in the world.

Elite companies such as Walmart, Exxon Mobil, Home Depot, and Target have all decided to have their shares traded on the New York Stock Exchange. It is very likely that when investing in stocks, the company that you have bought a piece of ownership in will be listed on the New York Stock Exchange.

The New York Stock Exchange has thousands of listed companies, and they all pay a pretty penny to have their companies listed and traded. In addition to that nice ransom, all listed companies have to meet strict requirements relating to the value of the stock, number of shareholders, and company earnings.

The majority of all companies listed on the NYSE are stable businesses, and the ones who lose their stability generally get de-listed or kicked off of the exchange. Stocks begin trading on the NYSE at 9:30 a.m. Eastern time and close at 4:00 p.m. The NYSE is open Monday through Friday and is closed for most recognized holidays.

NASDAQ

Behind the NYSE, I consider NASDAQ as the most prestigious exchange in North America and possibly in the world. Although it may have sounded like every big company is a member of the NYSE, there are many very high profile companies that are listed on the NASDAQ.

The NASDAQ is highly regarded as the exchange for tech stocks and is home to big names, such as Microsoft, Yahoo!, Intel, Cisco, and Apple Computers. Similar to the NYSE, there are very strict guidelines that must be met in order to be listed on the NASDAQ; therefore, most companies listed on the NASDAQ are quality companies in terms of having a certain level of income and assets.

During the tech boom in the late 90s and early 2000s, it was mostly companies that were traded on the NASDAQ that became extremely overpriced and were the reason behind the infamous bubble burst. A lot of these companies had stock prices that were rapidly appreciating, but the companies weren't making any profits. This definitely caught up to investors as the true value eventually came to light on many of these companies, and in some instances, the true value that was discovered was $0.

Types of Orders

Before making any investment decisions involving stocks, it is essential to know what type of orders can be made and how to read certain pertinent information that will be displayed to you when researching various companies' stock information.

First and foremost, it is important to know and understand some basic, yet important, terminology. When receiving a stock quote, there are generally three important things that you should want to know right away. The first is the current market price of the stock. This is established as the last price that the stock was sold for. When you hear that a stock is trading at $25 per share, this means that the last trade of the stock between a buyer and a seller was for $25.

The next two important things that you should know and understand are the "bid" and "ask" price. The bid price represents the highest price that someone is willing to pay for the stock at any given moment, and the ask price represents the lowest price that a seller is willing to sell the stock for.

Something very important for you to know is that, anytime the bid price is higher than the current or "last" price, someone is willing to pay more than the stock's current market price, which will raise the price of the stock to the latest purchase price if the person bidding was successful in buying shares.

Also, if the bid price is far below the "last" price, that means that the market is not in high demand of that particular company's stock, and if the stock is sold below current market value, the stock price will decrease as the value or stock price only represents the last price that the stock was sold for.

On the flipside, if both the bid and the ask price are far above the current market price and the two meet somewhere above current market value, the stock price will increase accordingly to what the last set of shares sold for.

When placing orders to purchase stock, there are many options that a person can choose from in deciding what type of order to make, and I'll be discussing the ones that I feel are important for you to know.

Market Order

A market order is the most common type of order in the market place. A market order doesn't request that the stocks be bought or sold at a certain price. It just asks that the transaction takes place at whatever the going rate is in the market place.

When someone makes a market order request, he is not concerned with buying or selling at a certain price and is generally comfortable with whatever the going rate is at the time of the request. For example, if someone makes a market request to buy shares of Home Depot and the going price is $29, then that is the price that he is usually going to pay.

Buy Limit Order

A buy limit order is an order that requests that the designated stock be purchased at a certain price or below. For example, if Walmart's stock is trading at $49, and an investor wants some but doesn't think it is worth more than $47, and not wanting to pay more than $47 for it, he or she can put in a buy limit order of $47. When the stock price dips down to $47 or below, the stock will be purchased for the going price as long as it is less than $47.

A buy limit order is a very good way to prevent from paying more than a certain price for a stock, especially if you've noticed a high level of volatility in the price of the stock and want to capitalize and buy it.

For example, if you noticed that Exxon Mobil's stock price constantly fluctuates from $65 to $67 on a daily basis and you wanted to buy some at the low point, then a buy limit order at $65 would buy the stock for you when it was again available at $65.

Sell Limit Order

A sell limit order is very similar to a buy limit order, but in this case, as the name indicates, it involves selling a stock instead of buying one. A sell limit order is a request to sell a currently owned stock at or above a certain price. This sell limit price is usually higher than the current market price.

For example, let's use help from the example above and say that after buying the Exxon Mobil stock for $65, you wanted to sell it as soon as the price went back up to $67 as you've noticed it's been doing for the last couple of weeks in your observations. In this case, you would place a sell limit order of $67, and as soon as the going rate was $67 again, your stock would be sold, therefore, making you a quick profit.

A sell limit order is a good way to sell a stock at a certain price without having to watch the market until it is paying a certain amount for the stock. With a sell limit order, you can just place it, and whenever the stock price goes back up, your shares would automatically sell if there are buyers in the market.

Sell Stop Order

A sell stop order is a good way to protect against losses when stock trading. A sell stop order is always placed below the current market price and triggers as soon as the stock reaches or goes below the sell stop order price. For example, if an investor owned shares of Apple and placed a sell stop order for $300, it would trigger and turn into a market order as soon as the stock fell to $300 or below. This would prevent the investor from taking any further losses.

Buy Stop Order

When short-selling, a buy stop order can be a good friend to an investor. A buy stop order is always placed above the current market price. It triggers and becomes a market order as soon as the stock reaches the designated price. For example, if an investor were to short shares of Google for $560, he could place a buy stop order to purchase the stock as soon as the price reaches or surpasses $575 or any other arbitrary number that he wishes.

Options Trading Basics

Options can be very risky if used the wrong way. They can also be very rewarding if used correctly, similar to any investment, but it is much more serious with options as you could potentially lose more money than you can dream of.

Options are a very good investment if you are the one buying them and potentially suicide if you are the one selling them. On the positive side, purchasing the right kind of option can be like having insurance on your stock in case the price declines. Also, a certain option can be purchased on a stock that you don't own, and if the stock price rapidly increases, your option gives you the right to buy the stock at the low price that's agreed to on your option.

Let's take a look at some of the option choices out there and which ones to stay away from. If you go against what I'm about tell you, you may need more than this book to gain wealth as you may end up in a hole that is too deep to climb out of.

Call Options

A call option can be your best friend, but if used the wrong way, it can quickly become the greatest enemy that you ever had. A call option gives the owner of it the right to purchase (call) a specific stock at a certain price (strike price), no matter what the current value of it is.

For example, if I own a call option on Nike stock with a strike price of $30 and the stock rises to $100, the person who sold me the call would be forced to sell me the stock for $30 even though it is now worth $100 per share. Obviously, this would give me a quick $70 per share profit without having much initial risk since I only paid pennies on the dollar for the option to buy instead of buying the stock outright.

On the other hand, the person who sold me the call option would be in a deep world of mess. If he owned enough shares of the stock to satisfy my order, he could just sell me his shares, but if not, then he would have to buy the shares at the current market price of $100 per share and then turn around and sell them to me for only $30 (my strike price) per share.

This could obviously put him in a horrible situation, and one that I don't ever want any of my readers to be in because it could turn out much worse than this. What if the stock price went up to $2,000 per share? The person who sold me the option would have to go out and buy enough shares to satisfy my request at the market price of $2,000 per share and then sell them to me at $30 (my strike price) and lose a ton of money in the process.

If the person owned the shares that he sold me the option on, instead of being forced to buy the shares at market price, he would lose out on what could have been a magnificent profit since he would have to sell me his shares at only $30 instead of being able to sell them at the current market price of $2,000 per share.

Like I said, a call option could be your best friend if used properly, so it is important that you understand how to use one. For example, let's imagine that you've been watching a certain company's stock and you believe it is getting ready for a strong upturn, but you're not sure.

Instead of buying 1,000 shares of the company's stock, which would be an expensive investment and a large risk, you could buy 10 call options (each option gives you the option to purchase

100 shares) that would give you the right to buy 1,000 shares at a specified price, so you can still profit from the stock's price gain (if it actually does increase) without having to actually own the shares at the time of the increase.

Put Option

Similar to a call option, if purchased, a put option could also be your best friend and used like an insurance policy for a stock that you currently own to protect yourself against a downturn. A put option gives the owner of a stock the right to sell (put) a stock to the seller of the put option at a specified price, no matter what the actual stock price is. For example, let's say I buy 100 shares of Walmart stock at $50 per share. If for some reason the stock price declined to $0, I would be at a loss of $5,000 unless I bought some "insurance."

If, in this scenario, I purchased a put option with a strike price (right to sell price) of $50 immediately after I bought the stock and then the stock price declined to $0, I would still be able to sell my shares to the seller of the put option for $50 per share; therefore, my only loss would be the price I paid for the put option.

In this scenario, the seller of the put option would be the one out of $5,000, minus the small revenue he received from selling me the put option, which would probably only be around $500; therefore, the seller of the put option would have a net loss of $4,500, and I would have a loss of only $500. This is good for me as I could have been at a loss of $5,000 instead of just $500.

As you can tell, buying a put option for protection is a great idea, while selling a put option to someone else can be a natural disaster waiting to happen. The thought of being forced to buy a stock for $50 that's no longer worth anything should show you the seriousness and potential dangers of selling put options.

Like with any investment, options can be good or bad depending on the level of knowledge of the investor. Also, one last note for selling call options is that they are particularly extra risky because there's no limit to how high a stock price can go, which gives the seller of the call an infinite amount of risk.

Fundamental Analysis

When investing in stocks, choosing wisely can be just as important as it is with purchasing real estate. Knowing when a stock is underpriced or overpriced can be a very powerful skill that can make or save an investor a ton of money.

There are certain tools that will be explained in this section that can be used in what is considered fundamental analysis. Fundamental analysis does not focus on the economy as much as it does the financial condition of a company and its stock price in relation to its earnings.

The following ratios are used in fundamental analysis to examine the condition of a company and its stock price to help an investor make a wise investment decision.

Earnings per Share (EPS)

The earnings per share figure of a company is closely watched by Wall Street and is used to determine if a company met its earnings goal and Wall Street expectations. A company's earnings per share (EPS) is calculated by subtracting money paid out for preferred dividends from the net income and then dividing the remaining figure by the number of shares outstanding (owned by the public).

For the sake of doing easy math, let's say that Nike had an annual profit of $10,500 and paid out $500 in preferred dividends. That would then leave $10,000 to be divided by the number of shares that are outstanding. Let's say that Nike only had 1,000 shares outstanding. That would then give it an earnings per share of $10 ($10,000/1,000 =$10).

Often, when a company's earnings are released on a quarterly basis, the EPS figure is usually what matters most to both individual and institutional investors. Generally, if a company misses its goal or comes short of Wall Street's (research analysts that cover and rate the stock) expectations for earnings or revenue, the stock price will immediately fall. On the other hand, if a company's earnings come back stronger than expected, the stock price will generally increase.

When earnings are equal to goals and expectations, the stock price usually isn't disturbed much since stocks constantly adjust based on what is expected of that particular company's earnings in the future. It is very important to know that a stock may have a large increase or decrease in price if the company, when releasing earnings, offers a future forecast of earnings that differ from analysts' expectations.

Price to Earnings Ratio

The price to earnings ratio of a company is also very heavily watched by Wall Street. A company's price to earnings (P/E) ratio is often used to measure if a company is trading for more than it is worth based on its earnings.

A company's price to earnings ratio is calculated by dividing its current market price by its earnings per share. For example, let's say that Nike was currently trading at $30 and had an earnings per share figure of $10 (based on example above for EPS). To find the company's price to earnings ratio (P/E), you would divide the $30 share price by the $10 earnings per share figure ($30/$10 = 3).

This would be a very attractive P/E if true. Depending on the industry and the potential for future growth that a company may have, a good investment usually has a low P/E of no more than 20. Otherwise, it may take a very long time before you see a satisfying return.

In some cases, a company's stock price might be low due to talks of bankruptcy or a possible government investigation on some of the company's practices. So just because a company has a high earnings per share figure and a low price to earnings ratio, it doesn't mean that you should automatically invest in that company. That would be an unwise business decision.

PEG Ratio

The PEG ratio is very important and is preferred by many investors and analysts over the P/E ratio to determine if a company is fairly priced. The PEG ratio divides a company's price to earnings ratio by its expected annual EPS growth. The expected growth rate used to calculate a company's PEG ratio is often based on one or five years. A PEG ratio of 1 or less is ideal. For example, if a company has a P/E ratio of 20 and has expected EPS growth of 20%, the PEG ratio would be 1. The only time I would recommend or consider buying a stock with a P/E ratio of more than 20 or 25 is if the expected growth rate meets or exceeds the P/E ratio.

Return on Equity

A company's return on equity is determined by dividing the company's net income by the shareholders' equity. This ratio is very important and measures how well a company has used its shareholders' equity to fund new earnings growth. The higher the return on equity, the better the potential is for share price growth.

However, as it is with other ratios, it is important to compare a company's return on equity only to companies in the same or in similar industries. Unless there is some reason to believe that a company has great unrealized potential, a 10% or higher yearly return on equity over a three-year period is required to spark interest in many investors who seek growth.

Debt to Equity

The debt to equity ratio is used to determine how leveraged a company is financially. It compares a company's debt to its equity. Companies are usually financed by issuance of stocks and bonds. The more bonds that are issued by the company, the higher its long-term debt will be. Although sometimes all debt is included, this ratio usually only considers long-term debt and divides it by the shareholders' equity, both of which are found on a company's balance sheet.

This ratio is imperative when considering the long-term viability of a company. When a company goes bankrupt, it is usually because of maturing debt that is unable to be satisfied or restructured. In some cases, the interest payments alone are so expensive that a company can't pay them and defaults on its debt, resulting in the need for bankruptcy protection. Also, when a company has heavy debt commitments, it is usually very hard for the company to grow since so much revenue is used to offset debt, and there often times isn't sufficient remaining capital for marketing, research & development, and asset acquisitions, all of which lead to growth.

Depending on the industry, a debt to equity ratio less than 0.33 is usually great, and a ratio of less than 0.5 is still very solid.

Current Ratio

The current ratio of a company measures its ability to pay its short-term obligations over the next 12 months from current assets, such as cash and cash equivalents. The current ratio is determined by dividing current assets as stated on the balance sheet by the company's current liabilities, also on the balance sheet.

A current ratio above two is considered satisfactory. However, what is considered satisfactory often varies depending on the company and industry. If a company has a current ratio of two, this would indicate that the company has twice as many current assets as current liabilities. If a company has a current ratio of less than one, this would indicate that the company may have trouble satisfying short-term obligations, all depending on how fast the company can turn over its inventory or raise capital.

Depending on the industry, a current ratio that is too high may indicate that a company has too many current assets and may need to do a better job of investing extra cash into higher earning assets.

There are many other ratios out there, including some that would be better discussed in an accounting book. I do feel that some are more important than others and, even further, that some are practically not important at all for the individual investor. A lot of these ratios are used by corporate executives to see if they are getting all that they can out of certain investments.

As a reminder, in addition to using these important tools of fundamental analysis, it is important to base your investment decisions on several other factors, including the business cycle you are in, the goals and objectives of the company, and your individual investment goals. These fundamental tools are just there to help you along the way.

Times to Invest in Stocks

Besides the abundance of opportunity with investing in real estate, another reason why stocks are not my favorite investment is because they do not make wise investments all year round and through every business cycle. Certain phases of the business cycle are much better than others for stock investing, and some are just horrible for investing in stocks.

Good Times to Invest in Stocks

The two scenarios that I find to be perfect for investing in stocks are at the trough (lowest point in the business cycle) and during certain parts of an economic expansion. The first scenario is during the lowest point in the business cycle, and that is because when you are at the bottom, the only way you can go is up. Generally, at this point in the cycle, all of the amateur investors have sold off all of their good investments for relatively low prices to astute investors who understand when to be greedy.

The second scenario is when the economy is going through a lengthy expansion with very low interest rates as well as little to no inflation. This is a perfect scenario as it usually indicates that the economy is flourishing and stocks will generally be the benefit. Usually in most expansions, the demand for goods is so high that inflation gets out of control, therefore, leading to rising interest rates.

So if an expansion is present with both low inflation and low interest rates, it is usually a great time to invest in stocks as corporate profits will likely continue to increase and set new earnings records, which normally will increase a company's stock price.

Bad Times to Invest in Stocks

As I said, not all times are good times to invest in stocks; actually, there are times that are horrible to take long positions in equities. Generally, during bad times to invest in stocks, you will hear people without a financial education talk about the latest stock that they've just purchased. When you hear this, it may be time to sell many of your stock holdings to the amateurs who are now entering.

Generally, it is well known that amateur investors jump into the market at the end of the up climb as they think they'll receive the same profits that were received by the people (astute investors) who bought the stock in the trough, when prices were at their lowest point. At this time, amateur investors are getting in at the stock's highest point, and once at the top, the only place to go is down.

When the economy is expanding (continually growing to new heights) and signs start arising that the peak is near and that a retraction is coming, it is usually a very bad time to invest in stocks. Generally, during an expansion that is nearing its peak, housing starts will begin to decline, and the Federal Reserve will usually raise interest rates in order to counter inflation that eventually accompanies an expansion.

Usually, the retail sales report will start reporting stagnate or declining growth when the peak is near. As stated earlier, consumer spending contributes to approximately 70% of the gross domestic product, which is the ultimate indicator of where the economy is. If the monthly retail sales report is negative two or three months in a row, you can be sure that the gross domestic product numbers will be negative or slowing for the quarter, and two consecutive quarters of negative GDP growth is an official recession. I'm not sure if this needs to be repeated, but this is usually a bad time to invest in equities.

Don't Even Think About It

The worst time to invest in a stock is when you receive an email or fax telling you that a company is getting ready to explode. This is often considered a hot stock tip, which is a scam 99.9999% of the time. No good company that is in a position to explode will need to do mass junk advertising of its stock.

Generally, when you receive one of these faxes or emails, it is from someone who is looking to inflate the stock price and then quickly sell his shares before the stock price drops back down to its true value, which is often $0.

Also, it is important to be careful whom you accept investment advice from as people who receive the "hot stock tip" will often give you the same advice that they have received in their email or through the fax machine without telling you where they got the information from. When it comes to buying stocks based on this information, do your family and yourself a big favor and don't even think about it.

Dividends

As briefly described before, dividends are the portion of company profits that the board decides to share with its owners (shareholders). When issued, dividends are usually paid on a quarterly basis. They are generally based on a predetermined dollar amount that will be paid for each share that you own.

Not all companies pay dividends as many of them need the profits for growing the business. Companies that usually pay high dividends are income companies that are already very large in nature and can afford to share their profits with the owners instead of using them for growing the company.

Most companies that do not pay dividends are small cap growth companies and mid cap businesses as they are all generally in the growing stage, and it is vital to use every dollar wisely or they may not survive.

Generally, retired and older people invest in income stocks for the income as they are too old to work and need the steady stream of income. Many others also invest in income stocks as some stocks are a mix of growth and income and provide an investor with steady income as well as an appreciating stock price.

Sometimes a company will decide to pay a dividend that normally doesn't. For example, in 2003, Microsoft, which was known as a non-dividend paying company, decided to pay an $850 million dividend to be divided between its shareholders as the company found itself sitting with over $43 billion in cash.

Once again, just because a company does one thing that you like, such as pay dividends, does not mean that you should automatically invest in it. That would be a very unwise decision and is a mistake that you should never make.

Stock Splits

There are generally two scenarios when a company will decide to do a stock split. The first will be to decrease the price of its stock to make it more attractive to new investors, and the other would be a reverse stock split to increase the price of a stock to make it more attractive.

The first scenario, which is to decrease the stock price to make it more attractive, would happen if the stock price has grown rapidly and the price no longer appears attractive to new and mainly amateur investors. The company would usually perform a two for one stock split. This would give all investors two shares for each one share that they currently own, and it would reduce the stock price in half. This doesn't add any profit or gain to the stock but only makes it more attractive.

For example, let's say that the high demand for oil raised Exxon Mobil's stock price to $150 per share. This price is considered relatively high, and the company would probably decide to do a two for one stock split. This would reduce the stock price to $75 and double the amount of shares that a particular investor currently has, which doesn't change the total value of the stock owned by the investor.

Let's say Denise owned 10 shares of the stock at $150 per share for a total value of $1,500. After the two for one stock split, Denise would then own 20 shares of the stock valued at the split price of $75 per share, leaving her total value at $1,500. The stock split only made the stock price more attractive to new investors.

The other scenario that would lead a company to do a stock split is if the stock price is relatively low and unattractive. This would be the case if the stock price is very low and nobody wants to invest in it because the public thinks the low stock price makes it appear that it is a poor performing company, which isn't always the case.

In this case, a company would generally do a reverse stock split. Let's say that because of all the losses and battles with union organizers that Ford's stock price decreased to $2 per share. At this point, many investors would think the company is getting close to being de-listed from the New York Stock Exchange and possibly headed toward bankruptcy. To help ease investor concerns, the company may decide to do a 1 for 10 stock split.

A 1 for 10 stock split would multiply the stock price by 10, making the value $20 per share instead of $2, and it would reduce or divide the number of shares owned by 10. For example, let's say that Tina owned 100 shares of Ford's stock at $2 per share, for a total value of $200. After the company performed the 1 for 10 reverse stock split, Tina would only own 10 shares of the stock that would be valued at $20 per share, therefore, leaving her total value at $200.

Stock splits are universally common for profitable companies during extended economic expansions when stock prices are generally rapidly increasing across the board. During the economic expansion of the late 90s, it was common for a growth or blue chip company to perform a stock split every few years to keep the stock price from appearing unattractive.

Day Trading

Day trading is very popular and is usually done by all types of people with all different goals. Some people's goals are to get rich quick, while others may be to double their $5,000 tax returns. Whatever the purpose, day trading can help you achieve your goals if done correctly, while if done incorrectly, as it usually is, can clean you out and make you wish that you never even heard of the stock market.

Day trading stocks can be compared to flipping real estate as you buy a stock at a perceived low price in hopes that you will be able to quickly sell it moments later or at least later in the same day at a profit. Sometimes this is achieved and sometimes it isn't, and it usually depends on the investment savvy of the day trader.

It is common and wise to day trade with stocks that have a large daily volume since all stocks don't trade large amounts every day, and it is hard to day trade with a stock that doesn't have a daily demand. For the record, most stocks that are traded on the New York Stock Exchange and on NASDAQ have pretty high trading volumes.

It is also very common to day trade stocks that fluctuate very often. For example, if a company's stock price went from $10 to $12 and back again on a daily basis for two weeks straight, many day traders will consider investing (or gambling) in this stock in order to take advantage of the large range of fluctuation.

Because day trading can sometimes be more emotional than rational, I do not recommend it to new investors as new investors usually haven't learned to control their emotions when it comes to investing their money. Learning to control your emotions in relation to your finances usually takes some maturing, losing money, and watching the cycle of stock prices as well as the economy.

Usually, I will only day trade unintentionally as I might buy a company that increases dramatically in value that same day, which will entice me to sell and take my quick profit. However, I am a huge fan of short-term trading. In this practice, I buy or short a stock the day before its earnings are scheduled to be released.

Most of the time, however, I will either buy several call or put contracts instead of buying the actual stock itself; therefore, I limit my exposure to risk and have the ability to profit if the stock does move in the direction that I believe it will after the company's earnings are released.

I have had major success with these strategies, and I only recommend doing short-term trading after the proper due diligence has been undertaken, which should include, at a minimum, studying any available market commentary on the stock, the company's finances, and its previous press releases.

The biggest reason why I don't recommend day trading for new investors is because many times an amateur investor will buy a company with the purpose of day trading that he would not have purchased if he were not intending to day trade.

I truly believe that everyone, at least subconsciously, has some sort of investment philosophy. A lot of times when attempting to day trade, people will completely disregard their philosophy when greed takes over and a chance for a quick profit is hoped for.

I can definitely testify to that since I lost several thousand dollars letting greed take precedent over my investment philosophy, which came from professional industry training of being a licensed financial advisor.

One day, I was watching the stock of a small cap company that was rising about 20% every minute for about 15 minutes straight. As the stock price climbed steadily, I became very tempted to buy and make a quick profit. A friend who was sitting at her desk next to mine even screamed at me to buy some, which was a totally emotional decision as she knew very little about stocks and investing. I broke my own rules and decided to buy some stock of a company that was rising rapidly but didn't have much revenue, let alone any profit.

It was a bad emotional decision that cost me thousands. About ten minutes after I purchased the stock, the price started to drop and it was decreasing at a much faster rate than it had increased. Before I was able to sell my shares, I had lost about 50% of the money I had gambled. So the moral of this story is to not make emotional investment decisions, especially when attempting to day trade, and if you're not 100% sure that you have your emotions in check, don't even think about day trading.

Last Words of Chapter

As I stated earlier in the chapter, investing in stocks can be a very important piece of a well put together investment plan if used properly. I do not recommend stocks as a main course to any meal (investment portfolio), just as society wouldn't recommend corn as the main course of a real meal.

They say knowledge is power, and with the information you learned in this chapter, you should be prepared to make some great investments. Just remember to do more thinking than feeling, and you should be all right.

Chapter 7

Investing in Bonds

When I was putting together the outline for this book, I was having a debate with key advisors deciding if I should include a chapter on bonds. I was having this debate because I'm not a big fan of bonds as I don't think they are a good investment for active and knowledgeable investors on their way to wealth but are much better for established individuals.

However, I don't want to confuse anyone into thinking that they (bonds) are bad investments because that's not the case. I just don't think that they make good investments for those who are not already established. Bonds are usually for those who seek income and less risk than those who invest in equities.

I don't necessarily agree with this 100%. I tend to follow Robert Kiyosaki's philosophy, and I determine the level of risk of a particular investment by judging the level of knowledge that the investor has on the particular subject. For example, if you know a ton about real estate investing, it should be very little risk involved for you. On the other hand, if you know nothing about real estate, your investing experience will be full of risk, and you may make a mistake that's hard to recover from.

What Are Bonds?

A bond, which may be referred to as a note or bill depending on its length, is a contract between the issuer and the investor. The investor loans money to the issuer, which can be a corporation, the United States government, or a municipal board. In return for borrowing your money to the issuer, it agrees to pay you a fixed amount of money, which is usually based on a percentage, for a certain period of time before it gives you your money back.

For example, let's say that Karen bought a Walmart bond with a face value of $5,000 (or five bonds in $1,000 increments) that pays her 5% a year for seven years. In reality, she loaned Walmart $5,000 for seven years, and Walmart is going to pay her a 5% yield each year for seven years. Each year for seven years, Walmart will pay her $250 (5% of $5,000) until the end of the seven-year period, and that's when Walmart will pay her back the original $5,000 that she loaned the company.

This picture does look a little better when considering much larger dollar amounts as shown in the next example. Let's say that Karen won the lottery and bought $5 million in bonds from General Motors. Let's also say that with all of the trouble that it's had lately, it has to pay investors much higher yields to compensate for the risk, and GM gave her a 9% yield on a seven-year bond. In this scenario, GM would pay her $450,000 (9% of $5 million) a year for seven years.

My strong opinion, which appears to be a dislike for bonds, is mainly geared toward investing small dollar amounts in them like the first scenario of Karen and only getting so little in return. I would advise someone with only $5,000 to invest in equities or to start a business.

Par Value of a Bond

The par value (which is also used interchangeably with face value) of a bond is the amount that will be paid to the investor when the bond matures. This amount is usually the same amount that was originally borrowed to the issuer by the investor but can be different depending on the terms that were agreed to.

For example, let's say Karen bought a five-year, $1,000 bond from Exxon Mobil with a 5% yield. In addition to the $50 (5% of $1,000) a year that she would receive from Exxon Mobile, at the end of the five years Karen would then receive her $1,000 in full that she originally borrowed Exxon Mobil. That $1,000 would be considered the par or face value.

Premiums & Discounts

Just as stocks can be traded on the open market, so can bonds. Also, just as the price that you sell a stock for may be different from the price that you paid, so can be the case when selling bonds.

Not all bonds that are taken out are held to maturity (the end of the loan period). In fact, many of them are sold on the secondary market at either a premium or at a discount, years before the maturity date.

When a bond sells at a premium, it is sold for more than the par or face value of the loan. For example, a $1,000 bond selling at a premium might sell for $1,200. Bonds are generally sold at a premium if the bond has a higher interest rate or yield than what is currently being offered on the market.

For example, If Karen purchases a $1,000 bond with a yield of 8% when interest rates are high, and then a year later the best rate being offered for new bonds is 5%, Karen would be able to sell her bond at a premium (for more than the $1,000 she paid for it) as it is paying a higher interest rate or yield than what is currently being offered on the market.

On the flip side of the token, a bond could also be sold at a discount. When a bond sells at a discount, it is sold for less than the face or par value of the loan. Bonds are usually sold at a discount when the yield (interest rate) on it is less than what is currently being sold on the market.

For example, let's say Karen purchases a $1,000 bond with a yield of 4%, and nine months later, the interest rate being offered for that bond is 7%. If Karen wanted to sell her bond before the maturity date, she would have to sell it for less than the face value as not too many people will want to buy a 4% bond for the same price that they can buy a 7% bond. It wouldn't make sense. She would probably end up selling her bond for approximately $900 since the 3% difference in her bond's interest rate (yield) and what the market is currently offering would cause for her to take a deep discount.

Bond Ratings

When investing, the reward of the investor is generally determined by the level of risk that is assumed. The higher the risk, the higher the potential reward must be and vice versa. If there is little risk for the investor, the investor generally gets little reward. This is true with most investments and bonds are no exception.

The amount of risk that the investor assumes when loaning a company or government entity money will determine the interest rate (yield) given with the bond. If the company that is issuing the bond has had losses over the last couple quarters, its bonds are considered riskier and must give higher yields (interest rates) to compensate for the high amount of risk.

On the other hand, if the U.S. government is issuing the bond, there is very little risk assumed by the investor as it is considered the most stable entity in the world. In this case, the investor would have to accept a below average interest rate since there is practically no risk involved.

To help investors measure the amount of risk associated with each bond, Moody's and Standard & Poor's are two very prominent companies that rate the quality of each company's bond.

These two companies generally divide the risk of each bond between investment grade and speculative. Obviously, the investment grade bonds have the lower interest rates, and the junk bonds have much higher interest rates to compensate for the additional risk.

With Moody's, the best grade that is given for the highest quality bond is Aaa, and then it proceeds with Aa, A, and Baa for investment grade bonds. Its junk bonds proceed in the following order: Ba, B, Caa, Ca, and C. The lower the grade, the higher the yield (interest rate) must be to attract investors.

With Standard and Poor's, the bond grades from best quality to worst are AAA, AA, A, and BBB for investment grade, and BB, B, CCC, CC, C, and D for junk bonds. Since they carry much higher interest rates than investment grade bonds, junk bonds are often called high-yield bonds.

Last Words of Chapter

When this chapter first started, it may have appeared that I was anti-bonds. The truth is that I am not anti-bonds, but I did make it appear that way intentionally. That is because there are much better things to do with your money if you're trying to build an empire.

Although I've gained a ton of patience over the last few years, bonds just move too slowly for me. I like money and I like it fast. Investing in bonds is not for a poor or middle class person as it will only help him stay poor or middle class.

On the other hand, if you are rich and want to live off of steady assets, I think bonds may make a very good investment for you if you're investing at least $2 million and receiving a minimum of a 5% yield. This way, you know to expect $100,000 a year for the life of the bond, and then you can expect to receive your $2 million at the end of the life of the bond.

Like I said before, investment choices should be decided considering all factors, including but not limited to, your investment goals, risk tolerance, ambition, and most of all your investment knowledge.

Chapter 8

Business Entities

Besides the investing techniques discussed in earlier chapters, there are many other legitimate ways to build wealth in this country, and the most famous strategy is by starting your own business. Not everyone is willing take this risk as the level of risk is directly correlated to the high potential for reward.

In fact, the definition of entrepreneur describes someone who takes a risk and starts a business. So it isn't a secret that there is a big risk starting a business, and it also isn't a secret that many of the richest men in the world are entrepreneurs, namely Bill Gates with Microsoft and Steven Jobs with Apple.

As I stated in an earlier chapter, I believe that the level of risk associated with something all depends on the level of knowledge the investor has in that particular business or investment. For example, if the founder of Nike decided to start another shoe company, it wouldn't be very much of a risk to him since he has the experience from building one of the largest shoe companies in the world. While at the same time, if he tried to start a hair salon franchise, it would be much more risk associated for him as his experience level on this topic is likely to be slim to none.

Starting and building a successful business can be one of the most rewarding feelings that a person can ever experience. Building a profitable business gives a person great feeling of accomplishment and wealth that can be passed down from generation to generation.

However, all of this potential for reward does come with an equal amount of risk and a large potential for failure. More than half of small businesses fail within the first five years. This can be a very intimidating number to some people, while being used as motivation for others.

The chance for failure can be dramatically decreased with proper preparation before starting a business by doing research, shadowing other professionals in the industry, and definitely by reading all you can. I was taught when I was younger that proper preparation prevents poor performance. With this in mind, it is scary to think of all of the people out there who start a business without putting together a sound business plan (will be discussed in a later chapter).

Another thing that many entrepreneurs fail to do is select the appropriate business entity for their type of business. At first glance, this may not sound very serious, but it definitely is. Certain entities will protect your personal assets, such as your house and savings, while forming a business with other entities will put all of your personal possessions at risk in the event something goes wrong financially involving your business.

Selecting the appropriate entity is very important when attempting to build a successful business as it may protect your personal belongings from lawsuits, both righteous and unrighteous ones that may be brought against you and your business. Besides building a strong business plan (that outlines your choice of entity anyway), I believe that carefully selecting the appropriate entity is the most important thing for any entrepreneur.

In today's litigious society, there are thousands of lawsuits being filed daily. Some of these lawsuits are legitimate, while many of them are people just trying to get rich quick with a phony claim. Also, some of these lawsuits are being filed against the actual owner of the business, while many others due to the choice of entity by the entrepreneur are filed against the business only, and the plaintiff can't go after any of the entrepreneur's personal belongings.

A person's wife is not likely to understand why she has to give up her four karat wedding ring because of a lawsuit brought forth due to an act of negligence done by one of her husband's employees. Although this sounds horrifying, it is done constantly and mainly because of people not doing proper research and just forming the easiest entity there is, which is often due to a lack of patience.

Sometimes when a person wants to make money, he loses sight of everything else that he is involved in or becomes very limited in what he sees. This is especially the case with young entrepreneurs who have created a very good product or who have come up with a brilliant plan. After the concept of the business has been created, the entrepreneur will often see only dollars signs and the potential profits of the idea.

This causes many entrepreneurs to lose sight of some of the most important things when starting a business, namely putting together a solid, well thought out business plan and selecting the appropriate entity. When doing these two things correctly, it definitely increases the entrepreneur's chance for success.

To help you with this, I will give you a list and details of the most popular entity choices available, such as the C corporation, S corporation, limited liability company (LLC), general partnership, limited partnership, and the sole proprietorship.

C Corporation

What does Walmart, Home Depot, General Motors, Nike, McDonald's, Exxon Mobil, Intel, Microsoft, Target, Ford, Lucent, Oracle, and every other company traded on the New York Stock Exchange and NASDAQ have in common? The answer is that they are all C corporations.

C corporations are the most popular entity for large businesses and small businesses that plan to become large and publicly traded companies (those who sell stock to the general public). C corporations have several benefits over all other types of entities, but a C corporation is not for every business as some businesses will serve better as either a limited liability company (LLC) or S corporation.

One of the biggest benefits of a C corporation over all other entities is that the ownership (shares/stocks) can be easily traded (bought and sold) on the open market without any difficulty as long as there is a demand for the stock. This is the main reason why all of the large companies I named above that are traded on the stock market are C corporations.

A C corporation is considered its own separate entity and can do many things that a person can, such as buy real estate, buy other businesses, get credit cards, sue people, and at the same time be sued. Of course, a person or a group of people have to manage a corporation, but they are not considered to be the ones making the transaction when the corporation does something such as buy an investment property or sue someone.

Limited Liability

One of the best things about a C corporation is that it has limited liability. This means that the only risk an investor has when investing in a C corporation is the investment that he makes into the business. The owner of a C corporation cannot be sued for the negligent acts of the business or for debts of the business, unless the owner has agreed to be held personally liable.

Due to the limited liability factor, in the event of a lawsuit, the corporation is the proper defendant, not the actual owners of the business. This adds a great level of protection, as with some entities, all of the business's owners are held liable for any and all liabilities of the business and can be sued for personal belongings, such as their homes, cars, and life savings to make right for wrong doings or debts of the business.

To give you an example of how this would work, I will give you the story of Kya. Kya was a published writer for several magazines and she decided to start her own magazine called *My Life Not Yours*. Kya was smart and decided to seek advice from a business consulting firm. After telling the consultant all of her goals for the business, he recommended that she start a C corporation.

About a year into the magazine, *My Life Not Yours* had over 60 writers who wrote from time to time for the magazine. One month, a particular writer decided to write about a rumor that he had heard about a famous celebrity as if he knew it was true. The magazine was nationwide, and the article about the celebrity created a large negative buzz and was believed by the celebrity to be the reason why she didn't get a movie role that she had auditioned for.

This made the celebrity furious and she was determined to get some payback. The first thing she thought about was suing the owner of the magazine. When she met with her lawyer about the issue, the celebrity's attorney notified her that he would not be able to sue the owner of the magazine, but only the magazine itself because it had limited liability protection as a C corporation.

This, of course, made the celebrity even more upset and she decided to get payback by saying bad things about the magazine and its owner that weren't true on a late night talk show. After Kya spoke with her lawyer about the situation, he advised her to file a lawsuit against the celebrity for slander, asking for $5 million for the magazine and another $5 million for her personal damages.

When the celebrity heard about this she was enraged since she was personally being sued by both Kya and by the magazine. She had two slander lawsuits against her for the same action since Kya's attorney felt that the celebrity's actions hurt the reputation of both Kya and the Magazine.

Instead of turning this story into a long novel, the point of this story is to show how a corporation can be sued, how it can sue others, and how it provides limited liability protection for its owners.

Piercing the Corporate Veil

In some instances, the limited liability of a corporation and its owner can be disregarded. When the limited liability aspect of a corporation is disregarded, it is legally called piercing the corporate veil. Piercing the corporate veil means that the owner of a corporation is being held personally liable for the actions or debts of the business. This generally only happens in situations of misconduct where the owners have done something fraudulently, deceiving, or something that went against corporation laws.

Actions that can cause the allowance of piercing the corporate veil would include the owner commingling business and personal funds, deceiving someone into doing business with the corporation while thinking he is doing business with a person, and fraud. These are all common reasons that will allow piercing of the corporate veil and remove an owner's right to limited liability.

Taxation

As its own entity, a corporation must file its own tax return separately of the individual owners. Opposite of other limited liability entities, if a corporation takes a loss for the year it cannot pass that loss down to the company's owners and is only considered a loss for the business. Businesses that can pass down losses are considered pass-through entities, and the C corporation is not one of them.

Tax rates in which C corporations pay taxes on are generally a lot less than what someone would pay with a pass-through entity for the first $50,000 or so. An owner of a pass-through entity (if it has profits) would pay taxes at the owner's individual tax rate.

For example, as of 2010, for the first $50,000 in profits of a corporation, the tax rate is currently only 15%. The next $25,000 ($50k-$75k) would be taxed at 25%, and the next $25,000 ($75k-$100k) would be taxed at 34%. This will generally save a business a lot of money if retaining income as it is normally less than a person's individual tax rate, depending on the tax and spending agenda of Congress.

One of the downsides to the way corporations are taxed is the fact that they are often double taxed. What double taxation means is that a corporation must pay taxes on any profits it earns, and if the company decides to pay out any dividends to its owners, they will also be taxed on their share of profits received, therefore, causing double taxation.

This is very unfavorable among many entrepreneurs and is the reason why many of them stray away from C corporations until they are ready to go public or seek private capital. It is important to note that a business can start out as one entity and then switch to another with the proper filing of paperwork.

Forming a C Corporation

A C corporation is formed by filing what is known as the articles of incorporation with the Secretary of State. The articles of incorporation would include the company's reserved (reserved with Secretary of State to check for availability) name, purpose of the business, board of directors, and often the company's bylaws.

The bylaws of a corporation outline the rules of the business and how management is to handle corporate affairs, such as shareholder and board meetings. The bylaws also generally list the responsibilities of officers and directors and the proper procedure to remove them from office if ever needed.

Each state charges a different fee for filing the articles of incorporation, so it's important to get those numbers ahead of time from your local Secretary of State's office.

A resident agent also must be designated in the state that the corporation is organized in. The role of the resident agent is to accept lawsuits and complaints in case they are ever filed against your business. Many corporations use attorneys as their resident agents to assure themselves proper representation and response to any and all complaints.

The owner of a corporation could serve as his own resident agent if he lives in the state that the business is formed in; otherwise, an attorney is always a good option.

S Corporation

The S corporation is very similar to the C corporation. In fact, in order to have an S corporation, one must form a C corporation first. After incorporating into a C corporation, the business owner must then file form 2553 with the IRS in order to qualify for S corporation status.

As with a C corporation, an S corporation also has limited liability protection from debts and wrong doings of the business and its employees. The differences between an S corporation and a C corporation are noticed within its tax status and restrictions.

Tax Status

An S corporation is considered a pass-through tax entity. This means that only the owners of an S corporation file a tax return, which is opposite of a C corporation where the business has to file its own tax return.

All profits or losses of an S corporation pass down to its owners. This means that if the business takes a loss, actual or only on paper, the loss passes down to the owner's personal tax return. For example, let's say Lisa started a part-time business and formed it as an S corporation that had a loss of $50,000 its first year. Let's also say that Lisa still had her full-time job as an engineer that paid her $60,000 a year. Because of the pass-through tax status of an S corporation, after deducting the $50,000 business loss from her $60,000 salary as an engineer, she would only pay taxes on $10,000 of income as that would be her new adjusted gross income, minus or plus any other income or deductions. It is important to check with your tax consultant as there are often times restrictions on the amount of loss that can be deducted from personal income.

This is a good reason to form an S corporation instead of a C corporation as this is not allowed with a C corporation. A loss with a C corporation is considered a loss of the business and cannot be passed down to its owners.

S Corporation Restrictions

The S corporation has several restrictions that make it unattractive depending on the goals of the business and the way it is to be owned and controlled. The following are a few guidelines that may lead a person to form a C corporation or a limited liability company instead of an S corporation as originally planned.

1.) S corporations are not permitted to have more than 100 shareholders. This is one of the reasons a large business that has the intentions to go public (be traded on one of the major exchanges) should not form an S corporation since most publicly traded companies have millions or billions of shares available to the public to be traded (bought and sold).
2.) Corporations and many types of trusts may not be shareholders of an S corporation. This is another reason why a large company that plans to go public should not form an S corporation. A large public company's stock is usually purchased by other companies but cannot be if it's an S corporation. However, 501(c)(3) non-profit corporations are allowed to be shareholders.
3.) An S corporation may not have non-U.S. citizens as shareholders. This is another tough restriction of an S corporation since many times venture capitalists and other investors may actually physically reside in another country.
4.) An S corporation may only have one class of stock. It cannot have preferred and common stock. This is another pitfall of the S corporation as some investors will want to receive a different class of stock than the other investors but will be unable to do so in an S corporation since only one form of stock is allowed.
5.) Profits and losses of an S corporation must be split evenly based on the percentage of ownership. This means that if one of the owners owns 20% of the business, he can only receive 20% of the profits or losses of the company.

The S corporation definitely does have its benefits, as well as its potential cost, as forming one can heavily restrict who can invest in your business.

Limited Liability Company (LLC)

In my opinion, the limited liability company (LLC) is the best of both worlds. Out of all the entities it is my favorite one by far. The only time I wouldn't use a limited liability company is if I were getting ready to take a business public because I would be required to form a C corporation.

The limited liability company has the limited liability protection of the C and S corporations, as well as the pass-through tax status of the S corporation without all the crazy restrictions, giving it the best of both worlds. The biggest difference between a limited liability company and an S corporation is the way profits and losses can be divided.

As stated above, in an S corporation, the profits and losses must be divided evenly based on the percentage of ownership. For example, if Kate and Michael equally own an S corporation, they must split the profits or losses of the business 50/50. No other agreement would be legal even if in writing.

With a limited liability company, the profits and losses can be distributed in any way the owners please. Therefore, if a particular investor will only invest if he gets 50% of the profits for the first two years, but he only owns 25% of the business, with a limited liability company this is perfectly attainable as long as it's agreed to in writing.

This is a big advantage over the S corporation in addition to the lack of restrictions that are applied to the limited liability company.

Forming a Limited Liability Company

In order to form a limited liability company, one must file the articles of organization with the Secretary of State. There is a fee to file this and it varies by state. The articles of organization include the company's name, purpose, resident agent, and if the business is manager or member managed.

With an LLC, manager managed means that one of the owners will have executive power over the business, and member managed means that multiple or all owners will have executive power over the business.

The next form that must be put together (although not filed with the Secretary of State) is the company's operating agreement. The operating agreement outlines the rules for operating the business. It will generally list requirements for meetings, removing managers, process to transfer or sell ownership interest, and distribution of profits and losses. If the last part isn't included, profits and losses must then be divided evenly according to ownership percentages.

The limited liability company has a lot of benefits and can be the perfect entity depending on the goals and objectives of the business and its owners. Like I stated before, unless I plan on going public in the near future, the LLC is my business entity of choice.

Limited Partnership

The limited partnership (LP) in my opinion is a half good and half bad entity. A limited partnership is a business that has at least one limited partner and at least one general partner. The reason I say a limited partnership is half good and half bad is because only the limited partners have limited liability of personal risk, but the general partner is at total risk and is held personally responsible for any debts or wrongdoings of the business.

The general partner is the one who manages the business and has executive say over the business and its day-to-day operations. The general partner is usually the one who founded the business or in most cases was the primary investor. The general partners have no limited liability protection of personal assets and can be wiped clean if the business has a large lawsuit against it or debts that can't be paid with business assets.

The limited partner is considered a silent partner and has no say in the day-to-day executive activities of the business unless he is an executive employee of the business, which in that case can act in his duties as an employee.

If a limited partner becomes actively involved in the business, he can lose his limited liability protection since only a general partner has the right to be involved in the day-to-day management of a limited partnership.

The limited partner is usually a minority investor in the business and wants nothing to do with the operation of the business because he doesn't want to lose his limited liability protection.

To give a clear illustration of how this works, I'll give you the story of Bob and George. Bob and George had a great idea and they started a limited partnership. Bob was cocky because he had a degree and wanted to be in charge of the business and, therefore, be the general partner. However, George was street smart and knew that as the limited partner he would enjoy limited liability protection in case something went wrong, so he quickly agreed.

Six months into the business, one of their employees spit in a customer's face during a heated argument that Bob was in a position to prevent. The customer then filed a multi-million dollar lawsuit against the business and won in court as the incident was recorded on tape. As the general partner of the business, Bob was handed the bill as a personal debt while nothing was ever said to George about any debts. George as the limited partner was not at all personally responsible for any debts of the business.

Forming a Limited Partnership

To form a limited partnership, you must file a certificate of limited partnership with the Secretary of State. The certificate of limited partnership generally includes the partnership's name, exact description of the business, resident agent, general partner information, duration of the business, and reasons for dissolving the business.

A limited partnership must also structure a limited partnership agreement. The limited partnership agreement lists the duties of the general partner, the limited partner's voting rights, and guidelines for transferring or selling ownership.

General Partnership and Sole Proprietorship

A general partnership and a sole proprietorship are the most horrible business entities known to man when it comes to personal asset protection. A general partnership is a partnership with all general partners and no limited partners. So this means that everyone involved in a general partnership is at risk of personal assets being seized to satisfy the debts of the business; therefore, no one in a general partnership is safe.

A sole proprietorship is a one person owned business where the owner takes full personal liability for the business. With all the entity options available, I don't understand why people are still forming these two forms of business entities. In my personal opinion, a person should be committed for forming one of these, especially if the business will have contact with people.

Forming a General Partnership & Sole Proprietorship

DON'T FORM ONE!

Last Words of Chapter

When picking an entity for your business, it is important to choose one that will benefit your needs. If you plan to go public soon, it would be unwise to form a limited liability company or a limited partnership that can't be easily traded or exchanged on the stock market, unlike with a C corporation.

Also, one must consider the need for tax breaks and deductions to personal income if the business is expected to take a paper loss (a loss only on paper for tax purposes) or even an actual loss for that matter. Many things must be considered as a loss with a C corporation can't be passed down to personal income, but this can be done with an S corporation, limited liability company, or limited partnership. This can also be done with sole proprietorships, but due to the risk involved, I wouldn't recommend forming a sole proprietorship unless your life depended on it.

Remember to never form a sole proprietorship or general partnership. Also know that if you start a business with another person and haven't filed for a specific entity, you have automatically started a general partnership. Also, if you are starting a business by yourself and haven't filed for a specific entity, you have automatically started a sole proprietorship.

I don't usually give examples in the chapter summary, but this last point needs an example to make sure you're clear. Let's say you start selling candy out of your apartment. You don't think it's that serious, so you don't form a legal entity with the Secretary of State, and one of the kids that you sold candy to gets sick and dies. Guess what? You are personally responsible if found liable since you are operating a sole proprietorship by default.

In this case, if the family of the child decides to sue you, you can be wiped out of everything you have or anything you may gain in the future.

So remember, C corporations are good, S corporations are good, and limited liability companies are my favorite. Limited partnerships are half good and half bad, but general partnerships and sole proprietorships offer no protection and are tragedies waiting to happen.

Chapter 9

Preparing Business Plans

The rate at which small businesses fail can be an alarming number since small businesses are responsible for creating the majority of all new jobs (statistics vary by region and business cycle).

There are many reasons as to why small businesses fail, including but not limited to ignoring the competition, ineffective marketing, ignoring consumer needs, incompetent employees, poor location, cash flow problems, and procrastination on behalf of the management staff.

Of the reasons listed, the two that call for the most attention, in my opinion, are location and the lack of meeting consumer needs. Many entrepreneurs, when looking for a location to start their businesses, don't take into account such simple things as the area's traffic, which is vital to your success. You can have the best restaurant in the world, but if no one ever hears about it or at least drives near it, that business may be one of those establishments that fail within the first three to five years.

Also, an abundance of entrepreneurs don't take into account what the consumers in their area want to buy that's not already being provided to them at cost lower than their business can afford to beat. This also goes in line with ignoring the competition. For example, some small tire shops have opened up less than a half a mile from a Sam's Club. This makes little to no sense due to Sam's Club having tires that are priced far below what most small businesses can compete with, which is due to Walmart's bulk buying power.

For some reason, it is evident that a lot of aspiring businessmen don't take into account the simple things when considering starting a business and that is because they don't spend time doing or paying someone to help them prepare a solid business plan. Research shows that most people take more time to plan a vacation than they do to properly plan for their business, which is scary at the least.

Doing a thorough business plan would answer all of the unanswered questions that an entrepreneur must deal with, not to mention those questions that many times an entrepreneur wouldn't tend to even think of. A sound business plan should include the following sections that are complete and full of exact detail.

1.) Executive Summary: The executive summary explains the objectives, goals, and mission statement of the business. This is similar to an introduction as it will briefly discuss what's about to be read inside of the business plan. Generally, when looking for funding, if the executive summary isn't strong, the rest of the business plan will either not be looked at, or in a best case scenario, it will only be breezed through.
2.) Ownership & Management: This section provides details on the type of business and management team the company will have. This section is very important, especially with limited liability companies and limited partnerships that can have different forms of management and can be controlled fully by only one owner. In the case of an LLC, it will explain if it's going to be manager managed and controlled by one of the owners or member managed and controlled by all or multiple members.
3.) History of Company: This section gives details of the history of the business if there is one. Many business plans are done for new businesses, while others are done on businesses that already exist that need funding for growing or

just want a clear direction of where the business is going. This section will talk about past financials and any obstacles that the business has overcome that likely may reappear in the future.

4.) Products and Services: This section explains what products and services are being offered by the business. This section will also give information on the need for the product or service and any other reason why the owners of the business expect this product or service to be profitable. This section needs to be very detailed since most businesses live and die based on the product or service being offered by the business. If you don't have a needed or highly demanded product or service before starting a business, I recommend not starting one.
5.) Locations & Facilities: This section gives the location(s) of the business. This section is one of the most critical parts as location is one of the main focuses of any solid marketing plan. A good location could mean a lot of free-flowing business, while a bad location could be the downfall for a business with a great product or service. In business, your location needs to be visible as well as accessible by your target market (the specific people you are trying to sell to).
6.) Sourcing: This section explains the costs of the benefits being offered. It will detail the price that the business is being charged for manufacturing of merchandise or for services that are being offered on behalf of the business. This can be very critical also since if the price that you pay to bring a product to the market is more than what consumers are willing to pay, it is a recipe for disaster and should be spotted before investing thousands or millions of dollars into a business.

7.) Technology: This section explains if the business owns any patents, copyrights, or trademarks that will help the business become profitable. Often, the technology that the business has patented will be the difference from a successful business and one that can't keep good data of past customers. I say past customers because without proper follow up, that is what they'll generally become.
8.) Market Segmentation: This section divides the market place into workable segments. It should break down each niche or market that will be targeted by the business. It will describe the order of marketing attacks and the effect that each attack will have on the market. This is very important since if no market is targeted, often no market will become established.
9.) Industry Analysis: This section is one of the most important sections as it may tell you ahead of time that you shouldn't start the business or at least not in the location that you were considering. This section explains who the competitors are in your market as well as in the neighborhood of the business. Similar to what I said earlier, if you are starting a tire shop and when doing the industry analysis in your business plan you realize that Sam's Club is only a few blocks away, this should cause you to redirect your business plan and change locations. This section should show that you've thoroughly researched your industry and, hopefully, it's healthy and growing.
10.) Competitor's Buying Patterns: This section will explain the logic and reasoning to the competitor's buying style. This is very important as knowing what your competitors are doing right could help you do the same things right as well.
11.) Marketing Strategy: This is probably one of the most important sections of a solid business plan as it will

address exactly how you will make sales and ultimately profits. It tells how you will implement the focus of your business and get your product or service known to your target market and ultimately the entire world.

12.) Pricing Strategy: This section is generally combined with the marketing strategy as it shows the current price list and discount structure of the products or services being offered by your business. It will show proposed margins (difference between sale price and cost of item) as well as detail any loss leader items that will be sold below cost to attract customers into your business with the hope that they will do a lot of impulse shopping.

13.) Advertising Strategy: This section is also usually combined in the marketing strategy section. It will describe exactly how you plan to spread the news about your business and should include a close estimate of how much each action will cost and the exact dollars expected from each advertisement, which is also known as return on investment.

14.) Strategic Alliances: The strategic alliance section will show if you plan to join forces with another company in order to strengthen the position of your business. Aligning your business with another company can be a great benefit for you as it can expose your business to new markets that it may have never been exposed to.

15.) Break-Even Analysis: This section explains how much income is needed to recoup cost incurred. In a business that has a product for sale, this section will show exactly how many pieces are needed to be sold in order to cover costs and make a profit. This section should also estimate total expenses, revenues, and profits for at least a one-year period; however, estimations for three or five years may be more attractive to potential investors.

16.) Final Summary: This section wraps up the main details of why your business is worth investing into and why it will be successful. This section will be a reflection of some of the best ideas of the business plan and will remind the reader of every section that caught his attention.

Last Words of Chapter

Preparing a solid business plan is essential for any business that plans to grow and become successful. Many people think that a business plan is just to help them plan their business, but just as important, it will often tell them that starting that particular business is a bad idea and, if heeded to, will save the entrepreneur a ton of time and money.

Chapter 10

Marketing & the 4 P's

In my opinion, marketing is one of the most important aspects in building a profitable, world-class business for any entrepreneur and definitely one of the most critical sections in a solid business plan. If a consumer doesn't know to demand your product or service, he generally won't because he can't if he isn't aware that it exists.

Marketing is the tool that is used to introduce your product or service to the consumer and ultimately build a household brand name for that product or service. Some of the most reputable companies in the world have used solid marketing plans to build their brands and eventually place their businesses in a class above the competition.

For example, Nike, who is the largest athletic shoemaker in the world, got that way from great marketing and promotion. In the mid-eighties, Nike practically made Michael Jordan, who became the greatest player to ever play the game of basketball, the face of Nike. At the time, Michael Jordan gave Nike a reputation for helping athletes fly or stay in the air a little longer than everyone else. With that, Nike made a fortune with its Nike Air brand even if the shoe wasn't directly related to Michael Jordan.

Even if a person couldn't afford to get the Michael Jordan Nike shoe, he still wanted to be associated with Nike in any way that he could, and shortly thereafter, Nike was the shoe of choice for both young and old athletic consumers. Recently over the last few decades, Nike has done a great job of grabbing other talent, such as Lebron James and offering him a mega $90 million endorsement deal.

Many outsiders didn't understand why Nike paid him so much money, and that is because they didn't understand marketing and the importance of a business branding its product. Nike understands that even if the Lebron James shoe doesn't make the company $90 million in profit over the term of the deal, the company will make its profit off of the branding that he will continue to provide for the shoe maker in associating Nike with world-class athletes.

This concept will surely make Nike much more than $90 million over time and will be the main reason why Nike maintains its position as the number one athletic shoe maker. Many other shoe companies don't believe in paying top dollar for world-class athletes as they only consider what that athlete will provide as far as his or her particular shoe sales, versus the bigger picture, which is the branding effect the athlete's affiliation will have for the shoe company.

Understanding this concept is the same as understanding marketing. According to the American Marketing Association, "Marketing is the process of planning and executing the conception, pricing, promotion, and distribution of ideas, goods, and services to create exchanges that satisfy individual and organizational objectives." In my own words, marketing is the process of creating public awareness and acceptance of a particular product or service and, in some cases, an entire business.

It is important to note that marketing is more than just advertising, the same way that a house is more than just a kitchen. Advertising is indeed a part of marketing, but the concept of marketing expands far beyond just advertising, just as a house expands far beyond just a kitchen.

Target Market

When marketing, the main goal is generally to reach a specific market. A market can be described as a collection of existing or potential customers who have the desire and ability to buy a specific product or service. The specific market that is sought after by a particular business or marketing plan is considered the target market.

Many businesses start out with a single target market that expands strategically in order to gain a larger market share. A good marketing plan will state a least one target market as well as the effect that market will have on other markets once reached. Having a clearly defined target market is very important before starting any business, no matter if it is a product or a service that you need to sell in order to make a profit.

A target market should include a group of people that have the desire and ability to buy a product or service. For example, if starting a restaurant that specializes in low-fat hamburgers, the target market could be overweight consumers who may have a high demand or desire for such food items.

If starting a book publishing company that writes mostly business books, the target market could be business students and business schools as a whole. Once a target market is defined, the marketing plan should detail exactly how the product or service will get introduced to that market and what will be done to persuade that market that the product that's being offered is worth the price that is being charged for that product.

Many different strategies can be implemented in order to successfully carry out a sound marketing plan, such as mail advertising, internet advertising, telemarketing, word of mouth, and television commercials to name a few.

Generally, the target market of a business grows when the original market has been captured and the company is meeting the sales goals that were planned when the target market was defined. Often, a new market will be introduced unintentionally. This can happen in many ways, but generally word of mouth will be the cause.

For example, let's say the target market of a book publishing company was urban women between the ages of 15 and 24. Because of the known relation between women and men in this age group, unintentionally, males in this age group could become a new market as they become curious of what their significant others are indulged in. At this point, the company's marketing efforts would now expand to reach this male audience as well as the original target audience.

This could very well lead to another market being created as the younger brothers of the older members of the 15 to 24 crowd may become curious of what their big brothers are reading. This could then lead to a whole new entire market of middle school age kids reading books published by this company that started out with the single target market of urban females ages 15 to 24.

When it comes to defining an initial target market, it should be a group that will likely openly receive your product or service as well as a group that will have some sort of influence on another market. That way you can kill at least two birds with one stone and expand into other markets without any direct attempts to do so.

On the contrary, not defining a target market is generally a recipe for failure since if no clear market it targeted, no clear market will be sought after, possibly leading to a very ineffective marketing campaign and entrepreneurial effort.

The Four P's

One of the best known marketing concepts in business is the four P's. This is also commonly referred to as the controllable marketing factors as they are the aspects of marketing that can be controlled by a company's marketing department. Not all marketing factors can be controlled by a company as a lot of marketing is done by word of mouth, and consumer psychology or behavior often has a lot to do with consumer spending and awareness.

In business school, one of the first things learned in marketing class is the concept of the four P's. The four P's are product, price, promotion, and place. This is a very important concept as they're the only factors that can be controlled by the business with the product or service to offer. Some add a fifth element, which is packaging, but I consider that to be a part of the product.

Product

The product or service that a company has to offer will generally make or break a business. You can have the best advertising in the world, but if the product isn't any good, the product won't be purchased, and if it is, it will generally be complained about, and not only not purchased again by the person that originally bought the product, but also not bought by whoever was on the other end of the complaints.

The product or service that is offered is the vital point of any business idea. Before doing any type of business or marketing plan, a good product or service that has a high demand needs to be created. To keep it simple, without a good product, there is no business or at least there shouldn't be.

Price

The price of a product is very critical. Just as having a good product is very important, the price of that product is equally as important as a poorly priced product can be just as bad as having a poor product itself.

Many times a company will have a great product or service to offer but it will be priced without consideration of the spending ability of the target market. For example, if I were writing a book on the steps to escape poverty, it would be unwise to price this book at $39 since many people in poverty wouldn't be able to afford spending that much money on a book, especially when the need to get food is the more immediate concern.

On the other hand, a great product can be underpriced and cause a business to fail. When deciding the price of a product, one must consider all costs associated with producing and promoting that product as well as the contribution that the sales of that product will have toward the general overhead of the business.

When evaluating the price of a product, if it appears that the product needs to be priced at a cost that is higher than what the competition is currently selling the same product for, it generally is a strong sign that the business idea needs to be reevaluated. When this happens, it means that the consumer need that you are attempting to supply is already being met at a price that you can't afford to compete with.

Promotion

The proper promotion of a product is equally as important as properly pricing and having a good product. A business can have the best product at the lowest price in the world, but if no one knows about it, it more than likely won't sell since someone can't request what he doesn't know is available.

For example, I can have a car dealership that sells Cadillac Escalade trucks for $500. That's right, $500. This is obviously a great product at a ridiculously low price, but if no one knows about it, chances are that I won't sell any vehicles unless someone stumbles upon my car dealership by accident.

Proper promotion creates consumer awareness of a particular product or service that is being offered. This is very important because, as I stated earlier, a consumer can't attempt to consume something that he doesn't know is available.

Place

Similar to how having a good product with a proper price and having good promotion is critical to the success of a business, so is the importance of having the product in the right place. A business can have the perfect product, with a similar price, and great promotion, but if the product is not in a place where it can be easily accessed by the target market, failure may be right around the corner.

For example, if I were selling high end business suits targeted toward wealthy consumers, it would be unwise to only have this product for sale in the inner city as it would create a barrier and possible hesitation for my target market to access my product. Having a product in the right place is very important and can make or break a business idea or company as a whole.

When preparing a solid marketing plan, all four phases of the four P's must be heavily considered as not one element may be ignored or lightly regarded. We've seen how any one can make or break a great business concept even if the other three have been brilliantly put together.

Consumer Decision Making Process

When putting together a good marketing plan, it is very important to understand the psychology of a consumer as he decides to purchase a particular product or service. Many people don't think it's important to understand this, but they are tragically mistaken. If you know the process done by a consumer leading up to a purchase, with the proper marketing, one can easily interfere with that process and find a way to make his company's product or service the selection of choice.

The first step in the consumer purchasing process is that he recognizes that he has a need for a particular item or service. This can occur from waking up to the feeling of thirst, having a cough, finding an empty cereal box in the food closet, and many other things can trigger this recognition of a need.

After a particular need is recognized, consumers usually perform an internal search as they try to remember how they last fulfilled the same need when it emerged. If no good experiences can be remembered, the consumer will move on to do an external search and ask friends and family for information as well as seek other sources that provide information on the product or service that is being craved.

After the consumer has done his proper research either mentally or physically on the computer, he will compare all of his reasonable options and look for the best value and all around choice. I was once told in psychology class as an undergraduate student that a person decides to have a relationship with someone or something by evaluating the benefits, the cost, and the availability of competing relationships. This is very similar to what a consumer does at this stage in the process. It may only take five seconds, but subconsciously, all things will have been considered.

After evaluating the options available, the consumer will eventually come to a decision and make a purchase. At this point, he will then decide whom to buy it from, which is very important as a business needs to be ready to position itself to be the place where the product or service is purchased from. This isn't an easy task, but properly following the four P's will have a business at the top of a consumer's list.

After the purchase and consumption of a product, the consumer will generally create an opinion of the experience and store it mentally for later use when the same need reappears in the future.

Word of Mouth

Word of mouth marketing is probably the best marketing there is. Word of mouth has been the bread and butter for many companies, especially underground music labels that don't get much or any radio play or spins on urban networks like MTV. Believe it or not, word of mouth is practically inevitable since after a product is consumed, the opinion that is created is usually shared with anyone who will listen.

This is the case if the opinion formed is positive or negative. Generally, when the experience is negative, the consumer will tell many more people than he would if the experience had been a good one. It is sometimes true when they say that people feed off of negative energy.

80/20 Rule

The 80/20 Rule states that 80% of all sales and profits will come from 20% of the items or customers. This is very important to know as it helps you focus your business efforts on particular customers and products. Customers that do 80% of the spending deserve 80% of the attention from marketers and managers.

Likewise, an item that provides 80% of the sales should be given 80% of the attention and should be strongly monitored to make sure that it is always in stock. Although all customers are important and should be treated with respect, it is not wise to spend a lot of time on customers who don't have the ability to do a large amount of purchasing.

Last Words of Chapter

Marketing is a very important topic that must be covered before a company decides to open its doors for business. Without the proper marketing, although the doors of a business may be open, it is very likely that no one will enter as no one will probably know anything about the business or at least not what the business has to offer versus the competition.

If you define a target market and take careful consideration of the four P's, marketing can be the bread and butter of any business that has admirations to grow and become profitable.

Chapter 11

Human Resources

In my opinion, people are the best resource and most valuable asset when looking to build an empire. In order to utilize and make the most out of this resource, it is critical that you understand human beings for who they are, what they do, and what they believe.

We've all had our experiences with different types of people. Some we've enjoyed and others that we sometimes wish we never crossed paths with. Whatever the situation, it is very likely that we learned something from everyone that we have come in contact with, either directly or indirectly.

In life, we often have little to no choice regarding the people we come in contact with, while as an entrepreneur, the power is yours to work with only those who you are comfortable working with. I've often heard people say that they don't like to work with people. However, it is my belief that they just don't like the people that they've worked with. It's a difference and a very valuable one at that.

One of the benefits of being an entrepreneur is that you are the boss. With the exception of some government regulations and requirements, you can pretty much do business as you choose and can also choose with whom it is that you do business with.

I must note that I am not okay with any form of illegal discrimination, whether it is based on race, religion, gender, color, creed, age, disability, or anything else that the government has prohibited. However, the one form of discrimination that I can concur with is that based on character.

As an entrepreneur, it is essential to choose only the best people to work with as the wrong people will be your downfall every time.

I would prefer someone with a bachelor's degree and good character over someone with an MBA and bad character. The reason being is the power of synergy. Synergy is when 1 + 1 = 3 or 4. The two individual parts, when together, are greater than what they could have been individually.

For example, if Fred and Sam could each make $50,000 in sales on his own and together as a group they only make $100,000, this is not synergy. It is instead wasted energy. However, if when teamed up they could create $150,000 or $200,000 in sales, this is synergy as the sum of the two parts when working together is greater than the sum of the two parts when working individually.

People often only speak of synergy in positive terms, but it works just the same or even more powerful when working as a negative force. For example, if two employees of bad character could each discourage 10% of your workforce on his own, it is highly probable that together they could possibly discourage 50 to 100 percent of your workforce. So in this case, 10% + 10% would equal 50% or greater.

This is why only having people of the highest character on your team is essential. The best people will team up and ensure that your company is a success, while those of low character will team up and ensure that your company and its brand name comes tumbling down.

In order to understand people, you must first understand what drives them. With saying this, I am not speaking of the shallow things, such as cars and vacations, but the deeper forces that drive us deep down within our souls.

Maslow's Hierarchy of Needs

Abraham Harold Maslow was an American psychologist, who is mostly known for diagnosing the forces that drive human behavior. His theory, which is found in most psychology and some business textbooks, is titled "Maslow's Hierarchy of Needs."

The needs are listed in order of importance and his belief is that the more important needs are the priority to the person until fulfilled, and once fulfilled, the person shifts his priority up the hierarchy. From most to least important, the needs are physiological needs, safety and security, love and belonging, esteem needs, and self-actualization.

Physiological Needs

The most important on the list is a person's physiological needs. These needs would include food, water, shelter, and the ability to breathe. These needs must be met before a person thinks of where to go for vacation or finding new friends. Just think, if you were hungry and haven't eaten any food in days, how likely is it that you're going to worry about who likes you or even if you like yourself at that point? Your only mission is going to be to find food and to attain it by any means necessary.

Safety and Security Needs

After a person's physiological needs are met, it is human nature to then seek out safety and security. This only becomes a priority after the person's physiological needs are met because when a person is lacking food or the ability to breathe, he doesn't care about safety and he will often engage in unsafe behavior to fulfill his needs.

Safety and security includes safety from physical harm and sometimes may include being secured in one's financial space. It is true that it is difficult for people to reach their full potential when they do not feel safe and secure, especially in their homes and neighborhoods of residence. At this stage, a person's focus is generally on survival.

Social Needs

Once a person has a sense of safety and is secure in the space that he's in, human nature calls for him to focus on his social needs, which are also described as the need to be loved and the need to belong. This would include having successful friendships, family relations, and sexual intimacy. Although this is third on Maslow's list, I know personally of people who successfully bypass this step in order to reach levels four and five. However, since business is a team sport where synergy counts for actual points, those who have taken the time to develop meaningful social networks are often in a better position to succeed.

It is my belief that many people have given up on love and some even feel as if they are natural misfits in society. People who feel this way often feel that these needs are not within their realm of possible achievement. They often bypass this level and reach for levels four and five, some of which do so successfully.

Esteem Needs

Esteem needs are very important and would include the need to have a healthy self-esteem, confidence, and self-respect. In order to reach this goal, many people will join various organizations, write books, become preachers, basketball players, or anything else that can remind or inform them that they have value and are worth something. It is my opinion that you must first convince yourself that you are worth something before someone else can contribute to your self-esteem. If you strive to be a good person, both personally and professionally, and believe that you are, eventually others will see you as a good person as well.

Self-Actualization

This is a person's need to be the best that he can be. The need for self-actualization is probably what led Kobe Bryant, during his prime, to start his daily workout at 5:00 a.m. every morning. He believes that with enough hard work, there is no reason why he can't be the best basketball player of all-time. Many psychologists believe that in order for people to reach this level they need their aesthetic needs satisfied.

Aesthetic needs would include the need to be in the presence of beautiful things, such as nature or someone you find attractive of the opposite sex. It is my opinion that many business people with large ambitions will often marry beautiful women half their age even when it's questionable if the person loves them or not. This is because the person's beauty is an asset to them and may even provide a busy person with a peace of mind, which is often needed to achieve one's ultimate goals in life.

It is important to be aware of this hierarchy because it may give you the solution to why your top salesman is underperforming or why your secretary appears to be depressed or lonely. For example, if half of your staff is single, it may be a good idea to provide, as a fringe benefit, free memberships to online dating sites. This will increase the chance of having a happy workforce, especially if you know that the person's physiological and safety needs are already met.

When to Hire People

It is my strong belief that you should only hire employees when you need them. No matter the field of business you are in, if you can satisfy the demands of the business personally or with the help of your business partners, no staff should be hired.

This is very important to the success of your business because it is very possible that if you can handle the demands of the business on your own that there may not be enough business activity to create enough revenue to support a workforce. However, if you have so much business that you can no longer serve all of your customers on your own, it may be time to hire temporary, part-time, or possibly even full-time help, all depending on the specific situation you find yourself in.

Payroll Services

If and when you find yourself in a position where help is needed, I do recommend that you use one of the major payroll services offered through either Paychex or ADP. Both companies will print payroll checks with funds taken from the company's account and will subtract all appropriate taxes from the employee's check.

This is a very valuable service and should be used to keep the entrepreneur from spending time trying to figure out tax formulas when he or she should be looking for new business. It is important to remember that as a president of your own company, your time is valuable and should be used on tasks that will add significant value to the company.

Morale

In my opinion, the key to a successful business is having employees with high morale. When your employees have high morale, they will often strive and go the extra mile to impress management, to make sure customers are satisfied, and that their work is completed at a high level.

On the other hand, employees with low morale will often talk bad about the job, their co-workers, customers, and management. This will then decrease the morale of the employees around that associate and before you know it, no one is happy anymore. This is often a challenge that is not handled well by many business people.

The best way to overcoming these types of obstacles is to nip it in the bud. If you hear an employee speaking badly about management or the company, respectfully pull that employee to the side and find out what is bothering that associate.

The key here is to listen carefully. Also, do not attempt to minimize his feelings by making him feel as though what he is upset or discouraged about is unimportant because obviously it's important to him, and if it's important to him, it is important to you and your business since people are the key to your long-term success.

Also, try your best to respectfully minimize negative gossiping. Bad talk and gossiping in the work place are disasters waiting to happen. It's hard to have synergy in the work place if your employees don't like each other and can't wait to do harm to one another.

As an entrepreneur or executive, it is important that you play the role of a mediator at times and that you demonstrate leadership by positive example.

Last Words of Chapter

Be careful of whom you hire and then be even more careful of how you treat and respond to the needs of the people that you do hire. Your people are critical to your business and are your most valuable asset. Could Walmart be the powerhouse that it is today if Sam Walton were still alive and he alone were the corporation's only employee?

Chapter 12

Mergers & Acquisitions

After building a successful business, many entrepreneurs find themselves in a position where growth appears as if it would be more efficiently gained by either acquiring or merging with another company. Usually during downturns in the economy, there are very attractive acquisition prospects.

On average, more companies become strapped for cash in bad economic times but many have great technology or client bases that are worth acquiring and because of their financial concerns can be acquired at discounted prices. Perfectly healthy companies can also be purchased at deep discounts during bad economic times due to a lack of other buyers and, therefore, a lack of leverage for someone looking to sell.

When an entrepreneur or executive makes the decision to acquire or merge with another company, he will usually contact the target company's CEO and share his interest. In some cases, the target company's CEO is disinterested in talks. If this is the case, this would be the end of the process with this company. However, if interest is reciprocated, the two will usually meet to discuss ball park figures and, if all goes well, they will usually agree to continue discussions and negotiations.

At the early stages of discussions, the two will usually consent to a confidentiality agreement. This will prevent either party from revealing valuable information that's discovered in the negotiations and also will prevent either party from doing anything to alarm employees of either entity that the company that they work for is possibly being sold or may be merging, which may result in downsizing.

If preliminary negotiations are successful, the two will usually produce a letter of intent that may outline certain terms that have been agreed to and forms an understanding between the parties that they have agreed to continue negotiations. In an acquisition transaction, the seller will often give the buyer exclusive negotiation rights that prevent the seller from attempting to negotiate a sale to a different buyer while the buyer negotiates and performs due diligence.

The due diligence process will include substantial investigations into the respective businesses. This will include reviewing financials and, more importantly, hiring of a professional team that should at a minimum include lawyers, accountants, and investment bankers depending on the size of the transaction. After the CEOs agree on a final price and iron out the details, they present the agreement to their respective board of directors.

There are several M&A transactions that are worth discussing. In this chapter we will discuss mergers, asset acquisitions, stock acquisitions, and leveraged buyouts.

Mergers

In a merger transaction, two or more companies merge and become one. Mergers will often occur between firms of similar size as companies usually acquire companies that are much smaller and don't bother to merge with them since it dilutes the voting power of their shareholders. Sometimes, although two companies are disproportionate to each other in size or earnings, a merger may still take place if the smaller company has either technology or some other very important asset that the larger company has placed a very high value on.

Delaware Merger Process

Although processes may vary slightly by state, Delaware is the most popular state for M&A activity and is where most large corporations are incorporated. To perform a merger between two Delaware corporations, the board of directors of both corporations must pass a resolution approving the agreement of merger and must issue a statement declaring its advisability. After board approval, both corporations must submit the agreement of merger to their shareholders for a vote to ratify, which requires a majority of all shareholders who are eligible to vote. A summary of the agreement is filed with the Delaware Secretary of State and a certificate of merger is issued to the surviving corporation.

At closing, the surviving corporation issues a pre-determined amount of its shares to the shareholders of the dissolving corporation. The dissolving corporation transfers all of its assets to the surviving corporation, which assumes all debts and liabilities of the dissolving corporation.

This issuance of additional shares from the surviving company to the dissolving company's shareholders dilutes the voting power of the pre-existing shareholders of the surviving corporation, but the surviving company usually gains value as long as the dissolving corporation's assets and earnings outweigh its debts and liabilities.

Exceptions to Voting Procedures

If the shareholders of the surviving firm would have the same rights, preferences, and privileges post transaction and their shares are not diluted by more than 20%, the shareholders of the surviving firm would not have the right to vote to ratify the merger agreement. This is known as the 20% rule.

Short-form mergers provide for another exception to the voting requirements. A short-form merger takes place between a parent company and a subsidiary when the parent owns more than 90% of the voting stock of the subsidiary. If a subsidiary is being merged into a parent company, neither company's shareholders have the right to vote to ratify the merger. If the parent company is merging into the subsidiary, the shareholders of the parent company must vote to ratify.

There is also a holding company exception. When a company creates a subsidiary to act as a holding company and that subsidiary creates a subsidiary also, when the original corporation that created the first subsidiary merges with the subsidiary created by the holding company, shareholders of none of the three entities are entitled to vote.

Triangular Mergers

In efforts to minimize risk to the corporation, many times a company will create a subsidiary for the sole purpose of merging with a target company, which will result in a wholly-owned subsidiary of the purchasing company. This is good because in a traditional merger, the debts and liabilities of the target firm are assumed by the surviving corporation. By creating a subsidiary to merge with the target firm instead of merging with it itself, the corporation protects its most valuable assets against unforeseen liabilities created by the target.

Companies will either perform a forward triangular merger or a reverse triangular merger. A forward triangular merger occurs when a company creates a subsidiary and merges it with the target company, therefore, turning the merger target into a wholly-owned subsidiary. In this transaction, the created subsidiary would be the surviving company after merging with the merger target. In a reverse triangular merger, the subsidiary created by the purchaser merges into the target company. In a reverse triangular merger, the target company would be the surviving company after merging with the subsidiary of the purchaser.

Asset Acquisitions

In an asset acquisition, the acquiring firm uses cash to acquire all (or some) of the assets of the selling firm. The selling firm will continue to exist and its shareholders shall maintain their stock unless dissolved. If dissolved, the corporation will pass proceeds down to its shareholders by way of a liquidating distribution. In an asset acquisition, the selling firm retains all of its debts and liabilities.

Generally, no shareholder vote is required of the purchasing firm even if the purchasing firm issues its debt securities in lieu of cash to acquire the assets of the selling firm. The selling firm's shareholders must approve the asset sale, with limited exceptions.

In Delaware, shareholders of the selling firm are not entitled to a vote if post-transaction the company still has significant business activity. States that have adopted the Model Business Corporation Act use a 25% rule, which states that the selling firm's shareholders are not entitled to a vote if, post-transaction, 25% of the assets and pre-tax income remain.

After an asset acquisition has been completed, the selling firm usually demands a shareholder meeting to vote on dissolution. If the majority of shares that are entitled to vote approve the dissolution, the firm must then file a certificate of dissolution with the Secretary of State. The firm is then given three years to wind up the business, pay its liabilities, and distribute any remaining capital to its shareholders.

De Facto Merger

As previously stated, in an asset acquisition, the purchasing firm only buys the assets of the selling firm and the selling firm retains its own debts and liabilities. However, if the court rules that a de facto merger has taken place, the acquiring firm would be liable for the debts and liabilities of the selling firm as if the two firms completed a merger instead of an asset acquisition.

A de facto merger occurs when there has been a continuity of the selling firm. This is attained by using the same or similar management, personnel, assets, and physical location of the seller's firm. A de facto merger also usually requires the selling firm to dissolve, leaving only the purchasing firm, which in turn operates the seller's business as if there has been no change in ownership, management, or assets. In a de facto merger, the surviving firm assumes all the debts and liabilities of the selling firm, which is usually more than it bargained for.

Stock Acquisitions

In a stock acquisition, the acquiring firm buys the stock of the target company from its shareholders. The acquiring firm becomes the owner of the target company and the debts and liabilities of the target company remain with the target company since the only change is with ownership of the target company's stock.

Tender Offers

In a tender offer, a bidder who usually seeks control makes a public announcement that he is interested in buying the stock of a corporation for a set price if a minimum number of shares are tendered to a deposit agent within a certain period of time. Tender offers are made directly from the bidder to the target company's shareholders. Tender offers do not require board member approval. A bidder may use a newspaper ad or other advertising to notify shareholders that he is interested in buying.

To encourage participation from shareholders, the bidder will usually offer a premium for the shares. For example, if a company's stock is trading for $20 on the New York Stock Exchange, a bidder may offer $23 per share, which would be a $3 premium.

The laws regarding tender offers require that the offer remain open for at least 20 days and shareholders must have withdrawal rights co-extensive with the offering period. If at any point the bidder extends a price increase, it must also be offered to those who have already tendered their shares.

Leveraged Buyout

In a leveraged buyout, a company will acquire a controlling interest in a target company using mostly borrowed funds. The percentage of borrowed money used to acquire the target may be as high as 95% and in many cases is well over 60%. The assets of the target company are used as collateral on the financing. The majority of leveraged buyouts are done by private equity firms that receive most of their financing from institutional investors. The firms receive their financing by issuing high interest debt to institutional investors who customarily allocate a portion of their investments in high risk junk debt.

After buying a controlling interest in the target company, the cash flow from the target company is used to pay the interest payments on the debt issued for financing. This can be very lucrative as a small investment combined with borrowed funds can get a firm control of a company, and after making debt payments, substantial profits are often remaining. The purchasers in a leveraged buyout will often seek to increase profits, which may be done by cutting payroll if the firm is unable to increase revenues. For this and other reasons, many have bad feelings regarding leveraged buyouts since downsizing is often the result, especially during economic downturns.

If the company is acquired during a downturn in the economy, chances are it will be acquired at a discount. The perfect scenario for doing a leveraged buyout is to acquire a company with substantial assets, a large operating income, and one without substantial long-term debt. There are benefits to doing leveraged buyouts in both good and bad economic times. In good times, you are more likely to grow profits to help repay debt. In bad times, the purchase price might be a lot better.

For example, if a company had yearly profits after taxes averaging $10 million, the shareholder(s) may be willing to sell for $40 million in a bad economy. If 80% of the purchase price ($32 million) is financed with debt at 10% interest, the interest payments would be approximately $3.2 million annually, leaving excess income of approximately $6.8 million.

In a good economy, a company with similar profits as the example above may reasonably request as much as $70 million. A 10% interest rate on 80% debt financing ($56 million) would total about $5.6 million annually in interest payments, which is a sizable chunk out of a $10 million profit. However, in a good economy, if the business has unlocked potential, good management and marketing will usually create growth and that $10 million profit may reasonably be at $20 or $25 million by the third or fourth year.

Depending on the terms of the financing, the entire amount of the financing is due on its maturity date. In the best case scenario, an increase in profits will have allowed the firm to pay off the debt well before the maturity date.

Leveraged buyouts are not done by just anyone since institutional investors are very careful with whom they invest with and, therefore, require private equity firms which seek such financing to have an impeccable reputation concerning matters of business and finance.

Appraisal Rights

In Delaware, appraisal rights are given to dissenting shareholders in merger transactions and permit them to petition state court for a fair value of their shares in cash. To have appraisal rights, the shareholder must not have voted yes on the merger, must have been a shareholder on the date of demand for an appraisal, and must remain a shareholder on the effective date of the merger.

Each company participating in a merger must inform its shareholders of their appraisal rights. This notice is usually given along with the notice of shareholder meeting for a vote on the merger. The company must notify the shareholders at least 20 days before the date of the shareholder vote. Any shareholder who wishes to dissent on the issue of the merger must notify the company before the shareholder vote.

If the non-dissenting shareholders approve the merger, the company must notify the dissenting shareholders that appraisal rights are available, which must be within 10 days of the merger's effective date. A shareholder wishing to have his shares appraised must file a petition with the court of chancery within 120 days after the merger's effective date.

Last Words of Chapter

A merger or an acquisition can be a great way to expand your business. Also, a financially healthy company with a product or service that has a high demand can often be purchased using borrowed funds by established entrepreneurs and investors. It is worth mentioning one last time that the best investments are often available during downturns in the economy, so be prepared for the next downturn with cash in hand.

Chapter 13

2011-2012 Economic Outlook

The Great Recession, which ended in June of 2009, erased 8.75 million jobs in the U.S. alone. On February 4, 2011, the Labor Department announced, although later revised, that the unemployment rate unexpectedly declined in January to 9% from December's 9.4% rate, despite employers adding only 36,000 workers a month after adding 121,000. The most significant factor, in my opinion, to the decrease in the unemployment rate was the 162,000 people who said that they were no longer in the labor force in January of 2011.

Private employers, which exclude government agencies, added 50,000 workers in January of 2011, while state governments reduced workers by 12,000 and the federal government decreased its payroll by 2,000 employees. For all of 2010, the U.S. added over 900,000 jobs, which is minimal compared to the 8.75 million jobs the country lost due to the recession. However, I believe that 2011 will be a much better year for those who are seeking employment.

Considering monetary policy measures taken by the Federal Reserve and the tax-cuts extension signed into law by President Obama at the close of 2010, I believe that the unemployment rate will be reduced to around 8.5% before the end of 2011 and below 7.5% before the end of 2012. I do, however, expect that after a few months of continual decreases to the unemployment rate, many of those who have walked away from the labor market will return, therefore, causing an increase to the unemployment rate.

I expect that the overall economy, which grew less than 3% (based on real GDP figures) from the fourth quarter of 2009 until the fourth quarter of 2010, will grow approximately 3.5% in 2011 and maybe as much as 4.5% in 2012. Employment for 2011 and 2012 will significantly affect GDP figures since consumer spending accounts for approximately 70% of the economy; therefore, if the labor market doesn't improve as expected, it will likely lead to a GDP growth figure of approximately 3% in 2011.

I also expect that the stock market will produce significant returns in both 2011 and 2012. Assuming there are no major, long-term threats to the confidence of consumers and investors, I believe the S&P 500 will grow at some level above 15% in 2011 and probably above 12% in 2012. The Dow Jones Industrial Average, which closed above 12,000 on February 1, 2011, for the first time since June of 2008, should outperform the S&P 500 and may grow more than 18% in 2011. I also expect the Dow to outperform the S&P 500 in 2012 and grow at some rate above 15%.

During the recession, many companies learned how to efficiently spend every payroll dollar and have recently been able to beat analysts' estimates with regard to their earnings; between January 10, 2011, and February 5, 2011, 73% of the 287 companies in the S&P 500 that reported their earnings outperformed expectations. Although I expect the unemployment rate to decrease during the two-year period of 2011 and 2012, I don't expect corporate executives to hire at the expense of slimmer profits. Employees hired in 2011 and 2012 should expect to work harder than they probably have ever worked since employers will likely hire the bare minimum needed to meet demand.

Interest Rates

The Federal Reserve's Federal Open Market Committee will have a tough job for the next few years. The Federal Open Market

Committee must decide when, and how fast, to raise the federal funds rate above the near zero percent rate it currently sits at in February of 2011. Many factors have been blamed for the Great Recession, including the sub-prime housing crisis. However, I believe that the 17 consecutive increases to the federal funds rate, from June 2004 to June 2006, played a very significant role. The 17 consecutive increases came after a one-year period of keeping the federal funds rate at a four-decade low of 1% from June 2003 to June 2004.

It is my belief that the federal policy makers kept the key interest rate too low for too long and countered that mistake with another—raising the rate too quickly. In an extended period of low interest rates, it is reasonable to expect a bubble to be created. During the period prior to the Great Recession, the housing market was the bubble, and I do not believe that it was handled properly.

In June of 2004, the FOMC raised the key interest rate from 1% and made 17 consecutive increases through June of 2006 until the rate reached 5.25%. I believe that anytime a bubble emerges, the air in that bubble should be let out slowly but surely.

Between 1997 and 2006, the value of the typical American home more than doubled. In March of 2007, the Federal Reserve stated that inflation was its main concern; however, with a federal funds rate above 5%, which was accompanied with a housing bubble, it should have placed the housing market as its main priority and taken action more quickly to lower interest rates; however, the Federal Reserve didn't decrease the key rate until September of 2007, and it was too late to fix the problem that had been allowed to grow beyond measure. Once interest rates increased and housing values began to plummet, mortgage borrowers who had adjustable rate mortgages found it increasingly difficult to refinance and many sub-prime borrowers walked away from their homes altogether.

During the period of economic growth that I expect the U.S. to experience for the next several years, it is important for the Federal Reserve to carefully implement policy so that no bubble is allowed to grow large enough to drastically impact the U.S. economy. Also, if a bubble does form, it is of the essence that policy makers let the air out of the bubble slowly but surely.

Good Investments for 2011 and 2012

The housing market, which helped fuel the economic expansion that ended in the fourth quarter of 2007 and then triggered the Great Recession, is currently in bad shape and may continue to get worse until 2012; however, this is good news for long-term real estate investors. In January of 2011, the Commerce Department released its monthly housing starts report and revealed that housing starts fell in December by 4.3% to a 529,000 annual rate. Although the trough for the overall economy occurred in June of 2009, the trough in the real estate market has yet to occur as home values continue to decrease throughout the country. It is my strong opinion that 2011 and 2012 will be great years to increase long-term real estate holdings.

I also believe that equities will make for great investments in 2011 and 2012. With corporate earnings surpassing expectations and many quality companies selling at very low price to earnings ratios, the stock market should have an exceptional 2011 and a very good 2012. I expect large corporations to outperform smaller entities; therefore, large companies with low price to earnings ratios and exceptional management teams should be targeted for investment.

About the Author

LaFoy Orlando Thomas III, Esq., is a licensed Texas attorney, business consultant, and published business writer. His business experience includes management, financial services, real estate, and entrepreneurship. In addition to his J.D., he holds two business degrees with honors and has been studying business and finance since the age of 14. While an undergraduate business student, he became a licensed financial advisor with American Express at the age of 20. Along with business and finance, his passions include economics, politics, and the study and practice of law. Contact the author at lthomas@thomaslawpractice.com.

Referenced & Recommended Readings

Books

Irwin, Robert. *How to Get Started in Real Estate Investing.* New York, NY: McGraw-Hill, 2002

Kiyosaki, Robert. *Rich Dad Poor Dad: What the Rich Teach Their Kids About Money That the Poor and Middle Class Do Not!* New York, NY: Warner Books, 2000

Lereah, David. *The Rules for Growing Rich: Making Money in the New Information Economy.* New York, NY: Crown Business, 2000

McCrary, Stuart. *How to Create & Manage a Hedge Fund: A Professional's Guide.* Hoboken, NJ: John Wiley & Sons, Inc., 2002

Oesterle, Dale. *The Law of Mergers and Acquisitions, Third Edition.* St. Paul, MN: West, 2005

Reed, David. *Mortgages 101: Quick Answers to Over 250 Critical Questions About Your Home Loan, Second Edition.* New York, NY: AMACON, 2008

Skeel, David. *The New Financial Deal: Understanding the Dodd-Frank Act and Its (Unintended) Consequences.* Hoboken, NJ: John Wiley & Sons, Inc., 2010

Wilson, Gregory. *Managing the New Regulatory Reality: Doing Business Under the Dodd-Frank Act.* Hoboken, NJ: Wiley Finance, 2011

Recommended Websites

Bloomberg
www.bloomberg.com

Department of Commerce
www.commerce.gov

Department of Labor
www.dol.gov

Federal Reserve
www.federalreserve.gov

TD Ameritrade
www.tdameritrade.com

Yahoo! Finance
www.finance.yahoo.com

Made in the USA
Columbia, SC
21 November 2019

83556741R00104